Dinner With Dr. Reese

Written By:
Dr. Kevin Reese, PhD, PAS, INHC, DS

Copyright © 2023

Seven Thirty Enterprises LLC
Farmington, CT 06032

www.DRKEVINREESE.com

ISBN: 979-8-9860807-4-1

Disclaimer

Kevin Reese, PhD, PAS, INHC, DS is NOT a medical doctor or physician and does not diagnose, treat or cure diseases.

Dr. Reese is a head-to-toe healer and gives assessments, provides education and gives recommendations based on the belief that the human body is divinely designed to correct itself. The Peace Over Pain Clinic is a non-medical institution and does NOT accept insurance.

If you choose to take advice from this book, you do so at your own risk and on your own will.

Acknowledgement

This cookbook isn't possible without the work and blessing of Ryan Aleckszander and Chef Norman Goodies.

Their book, "Cooking Without the Bad Foods." was the inspiration.

www.notusbooks.org

Thank You

Dr. Kevin Reese has helped thousands of people reclaim their health since 2010. He has a PhD in nutrition and certificates in other modalities such as postural alignment therapy and detoxification. He's the author of 8 books and has appeared as a guest on many podcasts and media outlets. Dr. Reese is considered the ONLY head-to-toe healer in the world due to his ability to work with any non infectious chronic condition. His Reversal System has produced mind-blowing healing results which have been documented on video.

Jumpstart Your Head-To-Toe Healing Journey With The Dr. Reese Book Trilogy

-Available on Amazon & Audible-

Peace Over Pain explains Dr. Reese's head-to-toe healing philosophy and how his reversal system works

Reverse The Cause explains the root causes to almost every non infectious chronic condition from Dr. Reese's head-to-toe healing perspective

Dinner With Dr. Reese explains how to eat without the poor four foods

Dr. Reese LIVE

The Show Airs Every Tuesday
at 6pm ET On All Social Platforms.

Or Talk to Him Face-to-Face in the
Exclusive Zoom Room. The Link is
Distributed Via Our Newsletter.

Experience Dr. Reese's Long Form Educational Videos on Rumble & Youtube

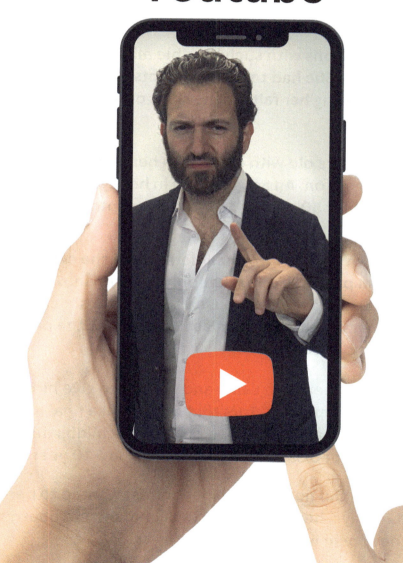

Grissel was on 16 medications with such horrible migraines that she couldn't leave the house for years. She had to turn the lights off and hide to let the "flare up" pass. After putting her faith in me she's only on 1 medication and has been pain free since 2017.

Linda came to us at 70 years old with nodules in her mouth that the dentist wanted to perform surgery on. An astigmatism in her eye. And she was chronically constipated for 50 years. All of these symptoms are now GONE after the reversal system.

Lorraine came to us with such frozen shoulders where she couldn't even wash her hair for 6 years. I'm pleased to say that only a month into our program she was washing her hair again in tears because it was such a shock. This emotional excitement inspired her to finish out her last 3 months of the program and lose weight and get out of more body pain.

Kim had a tumor blocking her birth canal and was set to give birth in 4 more months. Her medical monopoly doctors told her to make final preparations because she would more than likely bleed out during childbirth. Well, after 2 months with me, the tumor disappeared. Her son is now 10 years old.

Karen had horrible TMJ and neck pain so her dentist wanted to perform a $14k procedure. After 120 days, her TMJ is back in alignment and doesn't ache anymore and her neck pain has vanished.

Keysha had fibroids the size of grapefruits, psoriasis and migraines. 30 days into the program her migraines were gone. In another 30 days her fibroids shrunk to the size of golf balls. And 90 days in her nagging psoriasis was eliminated.

All Of Our Client Results Are Documented on Video!

Table of Contents

Higher Nutrition

All around the world, people are starting to heal by simply removing four food groups from their diet. As I describe in my book, PEACE OVER PAIN, I call these the "poor 4 foods."

Many of these people haven't even enrolled into my reversal system, they've only paid to read or listen to my book and have taken my recommendations very seriously.

While my reversal system is the only head-to-toe healing approach in the world, it's the first action step of getting off these 4 foods that starts the healing journey. Without the elimination of these foods, healing is hardly possible.

I assure you, there are plenty of foods left over. There are fruits, veggies (including potatoes), meats, eggs, beans, lentils, rice and fish. Nothing else is needed. This cookbook is my attempt to show you that it's possible.

It's time to drop the diet dogmas. It's time to drop the religion of keto, vegan, paleo, fruitarian etc.

The next time someone asks you, "what's the diet you follow." You can confidently reply, "I don't have a diet, I just don't eat the poor 4 foods." They will become curious and now you can educate them.

Be their teacher.

The POOR FOUR Foods

Gluten: Gluten is a protein found in wheat, barley and rye. It provides no essential nutrients and is known for intestine inflammation which interferes with absorption of nutrients. It typically increases appetite, raises blood sugar, contributes to ADD/ADHD and has a negative effect on hormones. Plus it enhances skin disorders, lung disorders and most certainly stomach disorders.

Oils: Oils are not a whole food and therefore becomes oxidized from the air. An example of oxidation is a cut open apple or avocado that turns brown. Oxidation creates free radicals which bond with cells in the body and then inflame them. Today's oils are very oxidized as they're processed, put in a bottle, transported long distances, then sit on a shelf at the store until you're ready to make your salad unhealthy.

Fried: There's a reason southern USA has the highest rates of heart disease and cancer. Overcooked food creates free radicals (carcinogens, AGE's etc) that slowly inflame the body. Once you eat something that turns brown, black or becomes crispy, you're basically smoking four packs of cigarettes per day.

Fake: If it's packaged in a box or bag, it's probably fake. Look at the ingredient listing and see all sorts of preservatives and dyes that break down the body. Over processed meat like sausage, bacon and salami also fall into this category. Real food only has one ingredient. An apple is one ingredient. Chicken breast is one ingredient. You get the idea!

www.DRKEVINREESE.com

The Slow Suicide

The side effects of eating the poor four foods is a very slow and tedious suicide.

Sounds dramatic right?

That's because it is!

You see, when we eat these foods, two major things happen to our bodies.

1- Our absorption gets blocked which means the essential nutrients are NOT being imported into our blood. This can cause up to 900 symptoms.

2- We increase free radical damage which creates inflammation. This leads to many chronic illnesses and eventually, the C-MONSTER.

It's this understanding that helps us stay off the poor four foods. Because if you don't understand, you'll keep eating them.

Example: When you were a kid and you touched a hot stove top, you came to the understanding that it's in your best interest to never touch it again!

The stove top is instant! Whereas food is a very slow deterioration process. This makes it harder for humans, especially when they're emotionally attached to the poor four foods.

For 2, 3, 4 or even 5 decades you consume the poor four and then you become a prisoner to the medical monopoly. Then your physician blames it on genetics.

Are the heart procedures, medications, dialysis and constant trips to the doctor worth it?

I take clients off the poor four foods right away. It's non negotiable. I will NOT take anyone's money that isn't ready to stop eating these foods.

No More Poor Four!

NO FRIED

-French Fries

-Fried Chicken

-Fried Eggs

-Tater Tots or any Fried Potatoes

-Veggie Stir Fry

-Potato Chips or any Other Kind of

Chip

-Well Done Red Meat with

Browning or Blackening on it

(charred)

-Burned Butter

NO OILS

-Olive Oil, Canola Oil, Coconut Oil,

Avocado Oil, Grapeseed Oil, Sesame Oil

etc

-This Includes Most Mayo & Dressings

NO FAKE

-Soda or any Carbonated Drinks

-Candy & Candy Bars

-Donuts

-Most Cookies & Crackers

-Most Cakes & Pastries

-Ingredients with Food Dyes

-Ingredients with 3 syllables

-Anything Hydrogenated

-Most Processed Meats Such as Bacon,

Sausage, Salami, Kilbasa or Cold Cuts

-Distilled Water

NO GLUTEN

-Wheat

-Barley

-Rye

-Oats

NOTE:
Oats do not
have gluten in it
directly but are
contaminated

Free Radical Damage

These invaders are constantly entering your system and causing inflammation through your breathing, eating, and drinking. They burn your cells. And this is arguably the largest factor in the cause of the C-monster. What to do?

We neutralize these free radicals with antioxidants. Antioxidants are qualified by an ORAC score (oxygen, radical absorption capacity).

Current research suggests that in order to extend our lives, we need 20,000 ORAC points per day. It's implied that the average American intakes, just 1500 ORAC per day, that's a huge gap.

Can you see why C-monster rates are so high? It's a battle between free radicals and antioxidants, and you do not want the free radicals to win. Think of free radicals as fire and antioxidants as water. If the fire is too big, it's going to be hard to put out the flames.

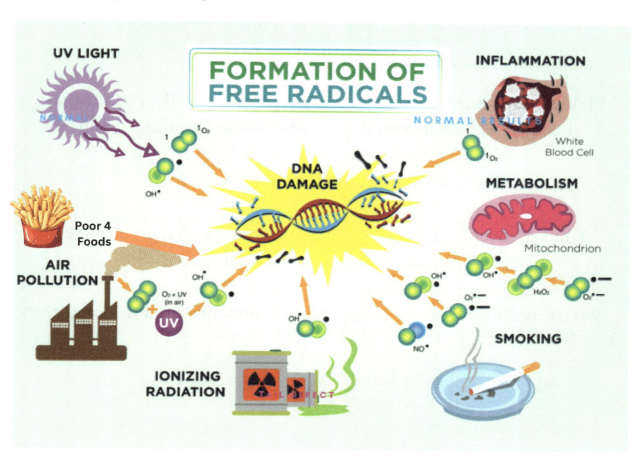

RED MEAT MYTH

Whether it's a passionate vegan or a medical doctor who was never trained to heal you, the word around town is red meat is bad.

This is false. Humans have been eating red meat for as long as fire was discovered. In fact, that is when human-beings started to advance.

Truly I tell you, with a very large nutritional profile, red meat is healthy, as long as you don't overcook it. Read that again.

Overcooking meat makes it a poor 4 food.

You see, overcooking fat creates oxidation which creates free radicals which creates inflammation.

So eat red meat rare or prepare it in a pressure or slow cooker.

YOUR COOKING METHOD MATTERS!

I cook with water. It's simple.

Best 3 Ways:
1- Steam Your Food
2- Boil Your Food
3- Pressure Cook or Slow Cook Your Food

But I understand that may be strange to you, so I'm giving you oven recipes in this book. Just don't burn!

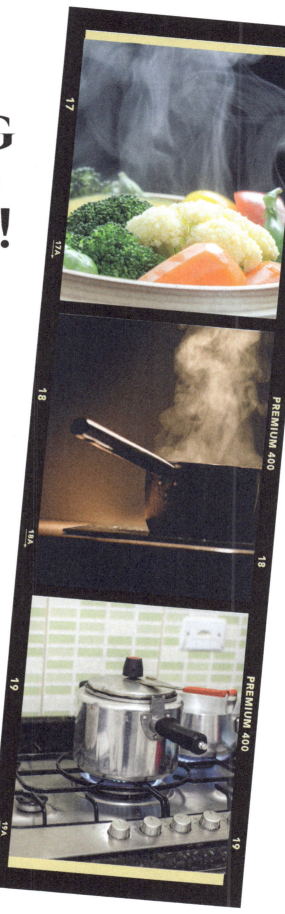

16

SALT ACTUALLY AIDS IN DIGESTION!

Salt your meats before cooking and then salt-to-taste after it's cooked.

NOTE:
Salt does NOT directly cause High Blood Pressure.

Nutritional deficiency, poor circulation and or high stress does!

STAY HYDRATED

Drink half your body weight in oz's of water. Go for more if you're sweating a lot.

Chug at least 8 oz when you wake up in the morning. Yes, CHUG.

Be sure it's NOT unfiltered tap water or water in a flimsy plastic bottle.

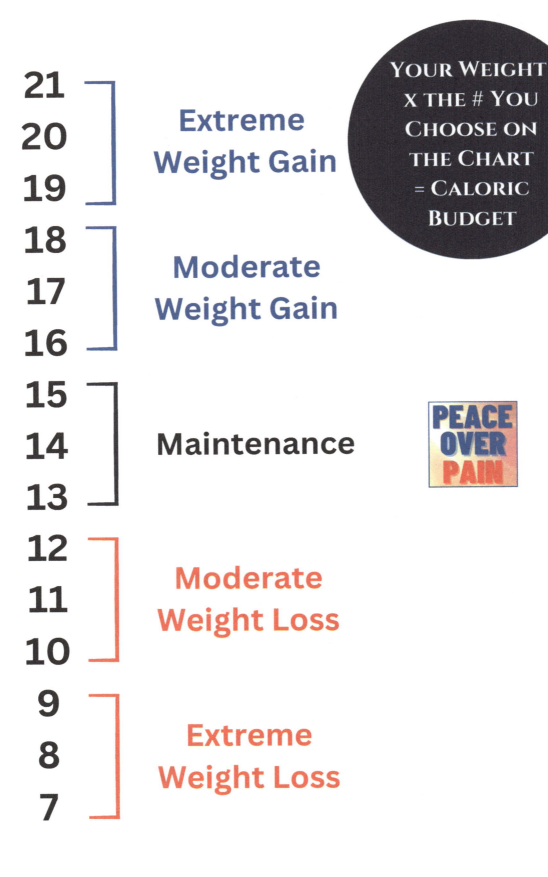

21
20   Extreme
19   Weight Gain

YOUR WEIGHT X THE # YOU CHOOSE ON THE CHART = CALORIC BUDGET

18
17   Moderate
16   Weight Gain

15
14   Maintenance
13

PEACE OVER PAIN

12
11   Moderate
10   Weight Loss

9
8   Extreme
7   Weight Loss

INTERMITTENT FASTING

**SCIENCE HAS PROVEN
FASTING TO HAVE AMAZING
BENEFITS.**

NO EATING FOR 12-20 HOURS!

YOU CAN DO THIS SIMPLY BY EATING 2 OR 3 MEALS PER DAY.

Example: If your last meal is at 6pm, then no eating again till 10am to make it a 16 hour fast! Keep drinking water.

BE SURE TO GET YOUR

90
ESSENTIAL NUTRIENTS

60 Minerals & Elements: Calcium, Magnesium, Phosphorus, Potassium, Sodium, Chloride, Sulfur, Cobalt, Copper, Aluminum, Arsenic, Barium, Beryllium, Boron, Bromine, Carbon, Iodine, Iron, Manganese, Selenium, Zinc, Cerium, Cesium, Chromium, Dysprosium, Erbium, Europium, Gadolinium, Gallium, Germanium, Gold, Hafnium, Holmium, Hydrogen, Lanthanum, Lithium, Lutetium, Molybdenum, Neodymium, Nickel, Niobium, Nitrogen, Oxygen, Praseodymium, Rhenium, Rubidium, Samarium, Scandium, Silica, Silver, Strontium, Tantalum, Terbium, Thulium, Tin, Titanium, Vanadium, Ytterbium, Yttrium, Zirconium

16 Vitamins: Vitamin A, Vitamin B1 (Thiamine), Vitamin B2 (Riboflavin), Vitamin B3 (Niacin), Vitamin B5 (Pantothenic Acid), Vitamin B6 (Pyridoxine), Vitamin B12 (Cobalamin), Vitamin C, Vitamin D, Vitamin E, Vitamin K, Biotin, Choline, Flavonoids and Bioflavonoids, Folic Acid, Inositol

12 Amino Acids: Valine, Lysine, Threonine, Leucine, Isoleucine, Tryptophan, Phenylalanine, Methionine, Histidine, Arginine, Taurine, Tyrosine

2 Fatty Acids: Omega 3, Omega 6

WE PUT OUR MEMBERS ON HIGH-QUALITY SUPPLEMENTS WHICH ADD UP TO THE 90+

Nutritional Deficiency is a Problem

Lack of the 90 Essential Nutrients. Plus Severe Deficiencies Hard Tissue Nutrients:
Arthritis, Back Pain, Bell's Palsy, Bone Spurs, Bone Fractures, Brittle Nails, Calcium Deposits, Cartilage Damage, Cognitive Impairment, Depression, High/Low Blood Pressure, Insomnia, Irritability, Joint Pain, Kidney Stones, Ligament Damage, Muscle Cramps, Nervousness, Osteofibrosis, Osteoporosis, Panic Attacks, PMS, Prolonged Blood Clotting Time, Receding Gums, Restless Legs, Tooth Decay, Vertigo

Lack of the 90 Essential Nutrients. Plus Severe Deficiencies of Soft Tissue Nutrients:
Acne, ALS, Alzheimers, Asthma, Blood Clots, Brittle Hair, Cracked Heels, Dementia, Extended Menopause, Eczema, Fibromyalgia, Fried Food Cravings, Gallstones, Growth Retardation, Infertility, Low Libido, Low Sperm Count, Multiple Sclerosis, Muscular Dystrophy, Psoriasis, Kidney Dysfunction

Lack of the 90 Essential Nutrients. Plus Severe Deficiencies of Blood Sugar Nutrients:
ADD/ADHD, Adrenal Failure, Anxiety, Bed Wetting, Bipolar Disorder, Cardio-vascular Disease, Depression, Diabetes, Elevated Cholesterol and Triglycerides, Fainting Spells, Fatigue, Hyperactivity, Hypoglycemia, Infertility, Learning Disabilities, Migraine Headaches, Moodiness, Narcolepsy, Night Sweats, Peripheral Neuropathy

Lack of the 90 Essential Nutrients. Plus Severe Deficiencies of Digestive Nutrients:
Allergies, Athletes Foot, Belching, Bloating, Gas, Burping, Celiac, Crohn's Disease, Dermatitis, Diarrhea, Diverticulitis, Food Sensitivities, Heartburn, Hiatal Hernia, Indigestion, Irritable Bowel, Leaky Gut, Acid Reflux, Stomach or Intestinal Pain, Yeast Infections

Going Gluten Free

Here's the problem with going GLUTEN FREE.

People are still emotionally attached to their starchy comfort foods!

The food corporations know this, so they've made all sorts of "gluten free" cakes, cookies, candies and bread.

But these gluten free "goodies" aren't good for you either!

In my book, Peace Over Pain, I lay out what I call the poor four foods. These are the four foods that slowly deteriorate our bodies by blocking absorption and creating free radical damage.

Eating these four foods manifest into nutritional deficiencies, inflammation and eventually the C-Monster!

The poor four covers a wide range and gets you off what you need to be off! Being just "gluten free' isn't enough!

For example, you could buy some gluten free bread, but it still has oil in it! You could buy some gluten free cookies, but it still has fake ingredients in it! You could indulge in some french fries which are gluten free, but they're fried!

Hahahah you're hit!

The best thing you can do is emotionally detach yourself from this "junk food."

It's time to ask yourself the tough questions....

Why do I love eating _____?
How does eating _____ make me feel?
Is it really worth eating _____ if I know it's slowly deteriorating my ONE body!?

If you're emotionally attached to certain foods, then getting off the poor four foods is going to be rough.

But I did it!

My clients do it!

Readers of the book across the world have done it!

You have to act like you want it.

Nutritionally Deficient?

Could I be nutrient deficient!?

I get asked this question all the time.

Well, do you have symptoms? If so, probably YES!

Here's the harsh reality. Our soil is depleted. It's a big problem in our new society. Something as simple as a carrot was healthier 200 years ago.

Keep in mind, farmers get paid by the volume, not by the nutrition. They don't care how much minerals are in your food, they just need to make a sale, just like any business.

Then there's gut issues from years of eating the poor four foods. It's not what you eat, it's what you absorb. So even if you're importing nutrients into your body, they're getting blocked!

Whether you're depleted because of farming issues or gut issues, it's a good educated guess that your symptoms are nutritional deficiency.

The problem is your medical doctor doesn't have clearance to run labs! They are merely soldiers in the medical monopoly! Health insurance will NOT allow them to check your full nutritional profile because it would cost too much money.

The solution - I always take clients off the poor four foods, work on gut health and get them on nutritional supplement protocols that supply all 90 essential nutrients.

It's so simple and easy!

The results make me look like a miracle worker.

But truly I tell you, It's just your body regulating itself. All you have to do is give it what it needs and take away what it doesn't want. Your divine design does the rest.

Why So Expensive?

Why Are Supplements So Damn Expensive!?

I get hit with this question a lot.

Some perspective....

I have clients that are on the bare minimum nutritional protocol which is about $150/mo. Then I have some that are on $600/mo protocols!

"What!? For some vitamins!?"

That's the response some people give. LOL

That response is all social engineering. You can tell because they used the word "vitamins."

You see, you have been programmed to hear the word "vitamins" these past 50 years and you've been trained to think of the cheap "multivitamin" from Walgreens.

Please note - There's ONLY 16 vitamins!

But there's 90 total essential nutrients your body needs!

Don't forget you also need 60 minerals, 12 amino acids and 2 fatty acids.

Each of the 90 essential nutrients can cause up to 10 symptoms. So that's 900 symptoms that can occur from nutritional deficiency.

There's 2 factors at play when it comes to the cost of the supplements.

1- What are your symptoms!? Some people are deeper in the gutter than others and it costs money to get them out. The best example is gut issues. Gut issues always cost more than any other because we need to get you on certain enzymes, flora, probiotics etc. There's a lot involved. Conditions like muscular dystrophy and the C-monster also are expensive.

2- How much do you weigh? The method of clinical nutrition is based on dosages. If you weigh 200 lbs or more, you're going to pay more because you will need to be on higher doses.

It's an investment for sure.

Think of it as health insurance. REAL health insurance.

Too bad your medical monopoly health insurance doesn't cover your supplements like it does your drugs right?

But why would the medical monopoly do that?

They want you to be sick so they can collect the health insurance money from doctor appointments, prescriptions drugs, surgeries, injections, dialysis, x-rays and more.

Can you imagine if you had to pay for all of that out of pocket?

It would make a $600/mo nutritional protocol look like a dinner at Applebee's.

Eating Out is Dangerous?

Wanna go out to eat?

Think twice about it.

We have been socially engineered that going "out to eat" is fun. It's social. It's a reason to get out of the house.

Here's the issue. It's very difficult to stay off the poor four foods when you're at a restaurant or cafe.

This is the one drawback of getting off the poor four foods. Even if you order a "gluten free" meal, you're still eating gluten.

Why? Because gluten can contaminate. So the gluten-based foods they have back there are next to your foods and it's getting on yours. You won't be consuming a high dose perhaps, but you're getting enough to perhaps screw up your absorption.

Then there's oils. This oxidized fat is their quick and easy way of making a profit. Restaurants are known for buying gallons and gallons of oils which is contributing to your free radical damage intake. Remember, a high-dose of free radicals can't be neutralized by antioxidants.

Fried is obvious, but fake isn't. Who knows what fake nonsense they sprinkle on this or spray on that. There's chemicals everywhere. Even the table salt could be the unnatural kind. Not to mention the tap water they serve you.

I understand the attachment. I used to practically live at Subway in my 20's and then Chipotle in my 30's. Then I woke up.

Here at the clinic, we advise our clients to stay AWAY from restaurants because it's much harder to escape the poor four foods.

If you want to heal the body or prevent your body from future dis-ease, then getting off these four foods are mandatory.

The solution is so simple. We teach our clients how to prepare food at home. This includes making easy and delicious meals in a pressure cooker.

However, social pressure will bring you to a resteraunt at some point. I usually tell clients to allow 2-5 restaurant visits per year and always order a rare steak cooked in butter instead of oils. Add a side of potatoes and veggies. Tell your waiter, you need a gluten free meal.

BEEF

RECIPES WITHOUT THE POOR 4 FOODS

PEACE OVER PAIN

BEEF STIR FRY

Ingredients:

- 1 LB of beef sirloin, cut into 2 inch strips
- 1 1/2 cups of fresh broccoli florets
- 1 red bell pepper, cut into matchsticks
- 2 carrots, thinly sliced
- 1 green onion, chopped
- 1 tsp of garlic, minced
- 2 tbsp of GF soy sauce
- 2 tbsp of sesame seeds, toasted
- Ghee or butter

Procedure:

- Heat a large wok or pan over medium high heat; cook and stir beef until browned, 3 to 4 minutes. remove beef and rest it. Add ghee or butter to wok and add broccoli, bell pepper, carrots, green onion and garlic to the center of the wok. Cook and stir veggies for 2 minutes.
- Stir beef into vegetables and season with soy sauce and sesame seeds. Continue to cook and stir until veggies are tender, about 2 more minutes.

80 Minutes

Serves 4

POT ROAST

Ingredients:

- 2 Lb of prime rib, chuck or rump roast
- 2 tsp of pink salt
- 2 tsp of pepper
- 5 to 6 sprigs of thyme
- 2 tbsp of garlic, minced

Procedure:

- The night before, rub the roast with salt, pepper, garlic and thyme, wrap with plastic wrap, and place in the fridge overnight.
- If the vegetables need some more cooking time, put them back in the oven and crank the heat to 350F/175C and continue cooking while your meat rests.
- Take the roast out about an hour before cooking, to allow the meat to come to room temperature.
- Once your roast has warmed, roast in the oven at 450F for 15 minutes, before turning the heat down to 325F for about 45 minutes to an hour (for a small 2 pound roast).
- Cook the roast until the internal temperature reaches 120F for rare or 130F for medium rare.
- Let the roast rest for 15-20 minutes before serving.

BEEF TENDERLOIN

Ingredients:

- 2 Lb of beef tenderloin roast
- 1 tsp of dry oregano leaves, crushed
- 1 tsp of course pink salt
- 1 tsp of black pepper, crushed
- 1 garlic clove, crushed
- 1 tsp of dry thyme, crushed
- 1 tsp of paprika

Procedure:

- Heat oven to 350F / 175 C.
- Combine all ingredients in a small bowl. Press combined ingredients evenly onto the surface of the beef tenderloin. Place beef on a rack in a shallow roasting pan.
- Place a meat thermometer in the center of the beef. Do not cover beef or place water at the bottom. Allow roast to cook for 35-40 minutes for medium rare.
- When meat thermometer reads 135F / 57C remove roast from the oven, cover it with aluminum foil and allow it to sit for 10 to 15 minutes. The temperature will rise to 145F / 63C allowing meat to reach a medium rare state. Transfer roast to a carving board and allow it to rest for 5 to 10 minutes before cutting. Cut into 1/2 thick slices.
- Arrange desired number of slices of beef on a plate. Spoon sauce over slices of roast beef.

20 Minutes

Serves 4

STEAK

Ingredients:

- A steak of your choice (ribeye, t-bone, porterhouse, new york strip etc)
- Pink salt (always salt your meat)

Cooking Levels Using a Meat Thermometer

- Rare: 125F / 52C
- Medium-Rare: 135F / 57C
- Medium: 145F / 57C

Procedure:

- Rest steak at room temperature for about an hour before cooking.
- Heat a heavy-based frying pan until very hot but not smoking.
- Add the steak, no seasoning.
- Sear evenly on each side for 2-3 minutes. This locks the juices in.
- Take the steak out of the pan and let rest for 10 minutes on a plate.
- Season with pink salt and any other seasoning you like.
- You could eat very rare at this point (use thermometer) or place in the oven at 425F for 5-10 minutes
- Serve the steak with the resting juices poured over.

BEEF JERKY

Ingredients:

- 2 to 3 Lb of lean round beef, flank or bison steak, cut into 1/2 strips
- 1 tbsp of pink salt
- 1 tbsp of garlic powder
- 1 tsp of fresh ground black pepper
- 1 tsp of onion salt
- 1/2 cup of GF Worcestershire sauce
- 1/4 cup of GF soy sauce

Procedure:

- Place strips of steak in a large bowl. Combine the remaining ingredients, stirring well. Pour over the meat, mixing thoroughly. Cover and refrigerate for 12 hours or overnight.
- In the morning, cover one of your oven racks with foil completely.
- Remove beef strips from marinade and lay on the top of the foil in a single layer. Turn on oven to lowest setting and leave door open 1 inch.
- Allow the steak to dry for 10-12 hours in glass tupperware and refrigerate. Place in freezer for an hour for easier cutting.

GROUND BEEF / TURKEY RECIPES WITHOUT THE POOR 4 FOODS

MEATBALLS

Ingredients:

- 1 Lb of ground beef or turkey
- 1 tbsp of onion powder
- 1 tbsp of garlic powder
- 1 tsp of cumin
- 1 tsp of paprika
- 1 tsp of cayenne pepper
- 1 tbsp of GF soy sauce
- Pink salt
- Black pepper

Procedure:

- Heat in the pan, medium low, add ghee
- Mix all ingredients together well. Really get your hands into it.
- Form golf ball sized meatballs, must be similar sized to cook evenly.

30 Minutes

Serves 4

SHEPHERD'S PIE

Ingredients:

- 2 Lb of ground beef or turkey
- 1 onion, diced
- 2 to 3 carrot, cubed
- 2 to 3 celery, cubed
- 2 to 4 garlic cloves, minced
- 3 to 5 potatoes, diced
- 1 cup of cream
- 3 tbsp of ghee
- 1/4 cup of GF flour
- 1 cup of beef or veggie stock
- Pinch of cumin
- Pink salt
- Pepper

Procedure:

- Start boiling water, cut the potatoes into the same size dice (same cooking time and doneness).
- Cook potatoes, drain, add cream and ghee. Whip it, whip it good. Salt and pepper. Set aside.
- Heat (medium) sauce pan, brown the ground beef/turkey and cumin (2-t minutes). Add onions carrots and celery. Add pinch of salt and pepper, Mix together.
- Saute' and marry all flavors, until high aromatic. Add GF flour, mix together well (you can brown the flour to add color to the gravy). Add stock, mix until smooth and watery consistency.
- Transfer to oven safe pan or continue in the cast iron pan.
- Scoop mash potatoes on the top of beef sauce. Spread evenly. Preheat 325F / 160C.
- Place in the own 25 minutes or until the top is browned.

CHILI

Ingredients:

- 1 Lb of ground beef or turkey
- 1 onion diced
- 2 to 4 garlic cloves, minced
- 1 tsp of chili powder
- 1 tbsp of taco seasoning
- 1 diced tomato
- 1 kidney beans (can or box)
- 4 cup of chicken or beef stock
- 1 tbsp of pink salt
- 3 cups of tomato sauce
- 2 tbsp of GF rice flour

Procedure:

- Cut onion, medium dice. Mince garlic.
- Add onions to large pot, start sweating. Add ground beef. Mix together then add garlic.
- Add all spices. Mix well, wait for aromatic then add tomatoes and kidney beans.
- Add stock, bring to a boil then simmer.
- Add tomato sauce continue simmering.
- Add GF flour in a bowl, take some hot liquid off the top of the chili. Mix with the flour until smooth, add back to the chili. Mix in, simmer for 20 minutes. Serve warm.

30 Minutes

Serves 4

HAMBURGER STROGANOFF

Ingredients:

- 1/2 cup of onion, minced
- 1 garlic clove
- 1 LB of ground beef/turkey
- 4 tbsp of GF flour
- 1 tsp of pink salt
- 1/4 tsp of pepper
- 8 mushrooms, sliced
- 1 cup of cream
- 1 cup of sour cream or greek yogurt
- 1/4 cup of ghee
- White or brown rice or GF pasta of choice

Procedure:

- Saute' onion and garlic in butter. Stir in meat and brown.
- Stir in flour, salt, pepper and mushrooms. Cook 5-10 minutes.
- Stir in cream and simmer, uncovered 10 minutes.
- Stir in sour cream/yogurt and garnish with parsley.
- Place on the rice/pasta and serve.

MEAT LOAF

Ingredients:

- 1 Lb of ground beef or turkey
- 1 onion diced
- 3 to 4 garlic cloves, minced
- 2 eggs
- 1 cup of GF breadcrumbs
- 1 cup of tomato sauce (oil free)
- Pinch of cumin
- Pinch of pink salt
- Pinch of black pepper

Procedure:

- Cut onions, dice. Minced garlic
- In a bowl, mix ground beef, onion, garlic and spices all together.
- Add eggs and breadcrumbs. Mix well.
- Preheat oven 350F / 175C. Place meat mixture into a loaf pan. Even it out, add tomato sauce, spread evenly. Place in the oven for 25 minutes. Depending on the thickness of meatloaf.
- Cut into loaf, serve warm.

38

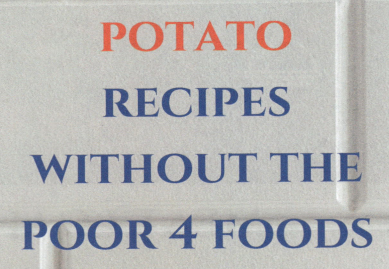

POTATO
RECIPES
WITHOUT THE
POOR 4 FOODS

CLASSIC MASHED POTATOES

Ingredients:

- 6 medium potatoes cut into 1 inch cubes
- 2 tbsp of sea salt for water
- 1 cup of half and half cream
- 3 tbsp of unsalted butter
- 1/2 cup of sour cream or greek yogurt, full fat
- 1 tsp of pink salt
- 1 tsp of ground black pepper

Procedure:

- Place the potatoes in a medium pot and add enough cold water to cover generously. Add 2 tablespoons of salt. Bring to a boil over high, reduce to a simmer, and cook, uncovered, until the potatoes are very tender and break apart with the light pressure from a fork. Drain very well in a colander. Return potatoes to the same pot to dry out for two minutes, over medium heat.
- Meanwhile heat together the half and half and butter in a small pan over low heat until simmering. Use a standard manual measure, breaking up the potatoes. Simultaneously add the hot cream and the butter inserts. Once the cream is fully incorporated, mash in sour cream or greek yogurt, and pepper. Taste and adjust seasoning as needed. stir frequently or keep warm for a water bath (double boiler) up to one hour. Add more sour cream or greek yogurt as needed.

25 Minutes

10 Portions

WHIPPED MASHED POTATOES

Ingredients:

- 4 lb of peeled baking potatoes
- 2 oz of butter
- 3/4 cup of milk or buttermilk (hot)
- Pink salt as needed
- Pepper as needed

Procedure:

- Scrub, peel and cut the potatoes into large pieces. Cook them by boiling or steaming them until tender enough to mash easily. Drain and dry. While the potatoes are still hot, mash or puree them.

- Add the butter and mix into the potatoes by hand or whisk until just incorporated. Add milk or buttermilk salt and pepper and whip it by hand or mixer until smooth and light.

45 Minutes

10 Portions

ROASTED POTATOES

Ingredients:

- 2 LB of red or yellow skinned potatoes
- 2 tbsp of butter
- 3 tbsp of chopped fresh herbs rosemary, parsley, thyme, dried basil
- 1/2 tsp of paprika
- Pink salt and black pepper as needed

Procedure:

- Preheat the oven to 300F/150C.
- Scrub potatoes and peel them. Dice into 1 inch cubes
- If time allows, soak potatoes in cold water for up to 1 hour. This removes starch and makes for a fluffier potato. Dry potatoes if required
- Toss potatoes, butter, herbs and seasonings
- Place on a baking sheet and bake for 40-45 minutes until browned or tender.
- Use any combo of herbs you'd like.

25 Minutes

Serves 4

BOILED POTATOES W/ GARLIC ROSEMARY BUTTER

Ingredients:

- 1 lb of small, round potatoes (scrub & clean)
- 4 tbsp of unsalted butter
- 2 to 3 sprigs of rosemary
- 2 to 3 garlic cloves
- Pink salt and pepper as needed

Procedure:

- In a large pot of boiling water, cook the potatoes until tender, about 20 minutes. Drain and half the potatoes.
- Meanwhile in the large pan, melt butter and add the rosemary and garlic.
- Cook over low temperature heat. Once aromatics have released, add potatoes for 2 minutes to be heated through. Serve immediately.

SCALLOPED POTATOES

Ingredients:

- 3 LB of potatoes, thinly sliced
- 1/2 onion, thinly sliced
- 6 tbsp of butter
- 9 tbsp of GF all purpose flour
- 3 cups of whole milk or as needed
- pink salt and ground black pepper to taste
- Chopped Parsley

Procedure:

- Preheat oven to 300F/150C. Grease a baking sheet with butter.
- Spread about 1/3 of the onion slices. Sprinkle 3 tablespoons of flour over the potato and onion. Arrange 2 tablespoons of butter. Season the entire layer with salt and pepper. Repeat layering twice more.
- Heat milk in a saucepan until warm. pour enough warm milk over the mixture in the baking dish so the top of the liquid is level with the final layer of potatoes.
- Bake in a preheated oven until potatoes are tender, 45 to 60 minutes.
- Add parsley to garnish

44

SWEET POTATO

RECIPES WITHOUT THE POOR 4 FOODS

PEACE OVER PAIN

30 Minutes

Serves 4

PEACE OVER PAIN

MASHED SWEET POTATO

Ingredients:

- 4 Lb of sweet potatoes
- 2 oz of butter
- 3/4 cup of milk or buttermilk (hot)
- Pink salt and pepper, to taste

Procedure:

- Scrub, peel and cut the potatoes into large pieces. Cook them by boiling or steaming them until tender enough to mash easily. Drain and dry. While the potatoes are still hot, mash or puree them.
- Add the butter and mix into the potatoes by hand or whisk until just incorporated. Add milk or buttermilk salt and pepper and whip it by hand or mixer until smooth and light.

45 Minutes

Serves 4

MAPLE ROASTED SWEET POTATO

Ingredients:

- 2 Lb of sweet potatoes
- 2 tbsp of butter
- 3 tbsp of maple syrup
- 2 tbsp of can sugar
- Lemon juice

Procedure:

- Preheat the oven to 325F/160C or set up a crock-pot.
- Arrange sweet potatoes in an even layer in a baking dish. Combine maple syrup, butter, lemon juice, salt and pepper in a small bowl. Pour the mixture over the sweet potatoes; toss to coat.
- Cover and bake the sweet potatoes for 15 minutes. Uncover, stir and cook, stiring every 15 minutes, until tender and starting to brown, 45 to 50 minutes more.

HASSELBACK SWEET POTATO

Ingredients:

- 4 small sweet potatoes
- 2 tbsp of butter, melted
- 3 tbsp of pure maple syrup
- 1 tbsp of fresh thyme leaves
- Pink salt and ground black pepper, to taste

Procedure:

- Preheat the oven to 325F/160C with an oven rack in the top third. Butter a rimmed baking sheet. Combine butter, maple syrup and thyme in a bowl.
- Working with one potato half at a time, place a wooden spoon on each side of the potato, and cut slits 1/4 to 1/8 apart crosswise down rounded side of the potato, using spoon handles as a guide to avoid cutting all the way through. Repeat with remaining potatoes.
- Transfer to a prepared baking sheet. Brush potatoes with maple mixture. Season with salt and pepper. Roast until golden brown and tender, 30 to 50 minutes.

35 Minutes

Serves 4

PEACE OVER PAIN

SWEET POTATO BAKED FRIES

Ingredients:

- 4 medium sweet potatoes
- 1/2 tsp of fine sea salt
- 1/2 tsp of pink salt
- 1/2 tsp of black pepper
- Extra salt for sprinkling over baked fries

Procedure:

- Preheat the oven to 350F/175C. Scrub then cut the sweet potatoes into 1/2 sticks. Add to a large bowl and add salt and pepper.
- Tumble sweet potatoes onto hot baking sheets and spread into one layer. Try not to crowd them too much or else they will not brown.
- Bake fries, turning once and rotating pans once, until edges are lightly browned and centers are tender; 15 to 25 minutes. The fries are done when the surface looks dry and the fries have puffed up a little. Don't worry if the edges become brown, they will taste more caramelized than burnt.
- Serve fries with a sprinkle of extra salt on top.

25 Minutes

Makes 3 Cups

SWEET POTATO TOMATO SAUCE

Ingredients:

- 1 LB of sweet potato, peeled, chop
- 1 tomato, chop
- 1/4 cup of heavy cream
- 2 tbsp of butter
- Pink salt and pepper, to taste

Procedure:

- Place the sweet potato in a large saucepan and add enough water to cover by 2 inches. Boil until tender, about 20 minutes. Drain and transfer the sweet potato and butter to a blender.
- Add the tomato, cream and puree until smooth (might need to thin out with a dash of water). Season the sauce with salt and pepper.
- Make ahead. The sauce can be refrigerated for up to 1 week or frozen for 1 month.

50

CHICKEN
RECIPES
WITHOUT THE
POOR 4 FOODS

15 Minutes

Serves 4

CHICKEN PARM

Ingredients:

- 1 lb of boneless skinless chicken breasts
- 8 oz of fresh mozzarella
- Pink salt and black pepper
- 1 cup of GF all purpose flour
- 3 eggs, beaten
- 1 cup of panko bread crumbs
- 1 tsp of garlic powder
- 1/2 cup of freshly grated parmesan, divided
- Ghee
- 2 cups of marinara sauce (oil free)
- 1/4 cup of thinly sliced basil
- 2 tbsp of chopped parsley

Procedure:

- Preheat oven to 425F. Using a sharp paring knife, cut a deep slit into each chicken breast. Stuff pockets with mozzarella then press edges of the chicken together to seal the chicken. Season outside of the chicken with salt and pepper.
- Put the flour, eggs and GF bread crumbs into three separate shallow bowls into the GF bread crumbs, whisk in garlic powder, dried oregano, 1/4 cup parmesan and 1/2 tsp salt.
- Dip the stuffed chicken in flour, shaking off excess, then dip the chicken into egg, tossing to coat. Dredge chicken in bread crumbs, making sure the chicken is evenly coated.
- In a large pan over medium heat, heat a thin layer of ghee. Add chicken to pan and cook until golden on both sides, about 4 minutes per side. Pour marinara around chicken and scatter basil on top of marinara. Turn off heat then sprinkle remaining parmesan on top of the chicken.
- Transfer pan to oven and bake until the chicken is cooked through, about 20 minutes more. Garnish with parsley and serve warm.

45 Minutes

Serves 4

CHICKEN CORDON BLEU

Ingredients:

- 4 skinless, boneless chicken breasts
- Pink salt and ground pepper
- 4 oz of preservative-free ham, thiney sliced
- 3/4 cup of dry GF breadcrumbs
- 1/4 cup of parsley
- 1 large egg
- 1/2 cup of GF all purpose flour
- 3 tbsp of butter

Procedure:

- Place a rack in middle of oven; preheat to 375F/190C. Trim any fat around edges of chicken working one at a time, place chicken between sheets of parchment paper and pound with a mallet or rolling pin until about 1/4 thick. Season chicken all over with salt and pepper.
- Arrange chicken smooth side down on a work surface. Cover one half of each breast with one slice of ham and one slice of cheese, leaving space around the edges. Fold breast in half over ham and cheese and press edges together to firmly seal.
- Combine breadcrumbs, parsley, 1 tsp of salt and 1/2 tsp pepper in a shallow bowl. Whisk egg and 1 tbsp water in another shallow bowl. Spread flour on a plate. Press both sides of chicken in flour, shaking off any excess, then dip both sides into egg mixture. Coat all over with breadcrumb mixture, patting with your fingers.
- Cook chicken, turning occasional, until browned on all sides, 3-5 minutes per side. Transfer to a wire rack set in a rimmed baking sheet; season with salt. Bake chicken until at instant-read thermometer registers 165F about 5 minutes.

CHICKEN SKEWERS
W/ AVOCADO SAUCE

Ingredients:

- 1 medium ripe avocado, peeled and pitted
- 1/2 Cup of Sour Cream
- 2 tsp of lime juice
- 1 tsp of grated lime zest
- 1/4 tsp of pink salt

Procedure:

- Flatten chicken to 1/4 thickness; cut lengthwise into sixteen 1" wide stripes
- In a large bowl, combine the lime juice, vinegar, chipotle pepper and salt; add the chicken turn to coat. Cover and refrigerate for 30 minutes
- Meanwhile, for the sauce, place the remaining ingredients in a food processor or mixing bowl until blended. Transfer to a serving bowl; cover and refrigerate until serving.

54

35 Minutes

Serves 4

PEACE OVER PAIN

GARLIC BUTTER BAKED CHICKEN THIGHS

Ingredients:

- 3 Lb (6 to 8) bone-in, skin on chicken thighs
- Pink salt and black pepper
- 1/2 cup of unsalted butter
- 5 garlic cloves, minced
- Zest of 1 lemon
- 1 tbsp of thyme leaves
- 1 lemon, cut into round slices
- 1 lb of baby potatoes, quartered
- 1 tbsp of chopped parsley, for garnish

Procedure:

- Preheat oven to 325F/160C. Season all over with pink salt and black pepper
- In a medium bowl, stir together butter, garlic, lemon zest and thyme. Rub butter mixture all over chicken thighs, including under skin.
- Place lemon rounds, potatoes, and chicken thighs on a baking sheet and bake until thighs register 160F/71C on an instant read thermometer, about 35 minutes.

20 Minutes

Serves 2

Sweet Sriracha Wings

Ingredients:

- 12 Chicken wings (about 3lb)
- 1 tbsp of ghee
- 3 tsp of ground coriander
- 1/2 tsp of garlic salt
- 1/4 tsp of pepper
- 4 tsp of butter
- 1/2 cup of orange juice
- 1/3 cup of sriracha chili sauce
- 3 tbsp of lime juice
- 4 tbsp of chopped cilantro

Procedure:

- Place chicken wings in a large bowl. Mix ghee, coriander, garlic, salt and pepper; add to wings and toss to coat. Refrigerate, covered, 3 hours or overnight
- For sauce, in a small pan, melt ghee. Stir in orange juice, chilli sauce, honey and lime juice until blended.
- Bake wings, covered, over medium heat 15-18 minutes or until juices run clear, turning occasionally; brush with some of the sauce during the last 5 minutes of cooking.
- Transfer chicken to large bowl; add remaining sauce and toss to coat. Sprinkle with cilantro and serve.

SALMON
RECIPES
WITHOUT THE
POOR 4 FOODS

PEACE OVER PAIN

HONEY GARLIC GLAZED SALMON

Ingredients:

- 4 (4 oz) salmon fillets, patted dry with a paper towel
- 2 tbsp of pink salt
- 2 tbsp of ground black pepper
- 1/3 cup of honey
- 4 tbsp of organic GF soy sauce
- 2 tbsp of lemon juice
- 1 tsp of lemon juice
- 1 tsp of red pepper flakes
- 3 tbsp of butter
- 3 garlic cloves, minced
- 1 lemon, sliced into rounds

Procedure:

- In a medium bowl, wisk together honey, soy sauce, lemon juices and red pepper flakes
- In a large pan over medium high heat, heat two tablespoons of butter. When butter is hot but not smoking, add salmon skin side up and season with salt and pepper. Cook salmon util deeply golden, about 6 minutes, then flip over and add remaining tablespoon of butter.
- Add garlic to the pan and cook until fragrant, 1 minute. add the honey mixture and sliced lemons and cook until sauce is reduced by about 1/3. Baste salmon with sauce.
- Garnish with sliced lemon and serve

58

15 Minutes

Serves 4

ASIAN BBQ GRILLED SALMON

Ingredients:

- 4 (4 oz) salmon fillets, patted dry with a paper towel
- 4 tbsp of hoisin sauce
- 2 tbsp of rice vinegar
- 2 tbsp of organic GF soy sauce
- 2 tsp of mirin
- 1/2 tsp of garlic chili paste
- 1 tbsp of minced fresh ginger
- Zest and juice of 1/2 a lime
- 1/2 tsp of garlic powder
- butter
- thinly sliced onions
- sesame seeds

Procedure:

- In a large bowl, whisk together hoisin sauce, rice vinegar, soy sauce, mirin, garlic chili paste, ginger, lime juice and zest, and garlic powder.

- Preheat grill on high and brush with butter. Place salmon fillets directly on grill, skin side down and cook for 5 minutes. Using a heavy-duty spatula, carefully flip salmon and brush with BBQ sauce. Cook another 2 to 3 minutes or until cooked through.

CLASSIC SALMON STEAK

Ingredients:

- 4 (12 oz) salmon steaks, bones removed
- 2 tbsp of pink salt
- 2 tbsp of ground black pepper
- 2 tbsp of ghee
- 2 tbsp of butter
- 2 garlic cloves, minced
- Juice of 1 lemon
- 2 tbsp of honey
- 1/4 tsp of crushed red pepper flakes
- Chopped parsley

Procedure:

- Season salmon on both sides with salt and pepper. In a large pan over medium-high heat, heat the ghee. Add salmon and cook until bottom is golden, 5 minutes, then flip. Add butter, garlic, lemon juice, honey, and red pepper flakes. Cook until salmon is cooked through, another 5 minutes, spooning sauce over salmon as it cooks.
- Garnish with parsley before serving.

15 Minutes

Serves 4

SALMON BURGERS

Ingredients:

- 14 oz of canned salmon, drained
- 1 large egg, lightly beaten
- 1/2 cup of GF bread crumbs
- 1 garlic clove, minced
- Zest and juice of 1 lemon
- 3 tbsp of chopped dill
- 1 tbsp of dijon mustard
- 1/2 tsp of red pepper flakes
- 2 tbsp of pink salt
- 2 tbsp of ground black pepper
- 1 tbsp of ghee

Procedure:

- In a large bowl, combine salmon with egg, GF bread crumbs, garlic, lemon zest and juice, dill, dijon, and red pepper flakes. Season with salt and pepper and stir until fully combined, then form into 3 to 4 patties.
- In a large pan, heat ghee. Add patties and cook until golden, about 4 minutes on each side.
- Serve regular or on GF buns.

15 Minutes

Serves 4

PEACE OVER PAIN

SALMON PICCATA

Ingredients:

- 4 (8 oz) salmon fillets
- 2 tbsp of pink salt
- 2 tbsp of ground black pepper
- 1/2 cup GF flour of choice
- 2 tbsp of ghee
- 3 tbsp of butter
- 2 garlic cloves, minced
- 1/4 cup of capers
- 2 tbsp of finely chopped sun-dried tomatoes
- 2 tbsp of chopped parsley

Procedure:

- Season salmon fillets with salt and pepper and dredge in flour, shaking off any excess flour.
- In a large pan over medium heat, heat ghee. Sear salmon until golden on both sides, 4 to 5 minutes a side. Transfer salmon to plate and tent with foil to keep warm while making sauce.
- Melt butter in pan and stir in garlic. Cook until fragrant, 1 to 2 minutes, then stir in flour. Cook 1 to 2 minutes more, until lightly golden in color and bubbling slightly. Slowly whisk in wine to de-glaze, scraping up any brown bits left on the bottom of the pan. Whisk in chicken stock and bring to a simmer and cook until thickened slightly, 4 to 5 minutes. Stir in lemon juice, lemon slices, caper and sun dried tomatoes and season to taste with salt and pepper.
- Return salmon to pan and let simmer in the sauce. Spoon sauce over salmon and let cook 3 to 4 minutes more. Garnish with parsley.

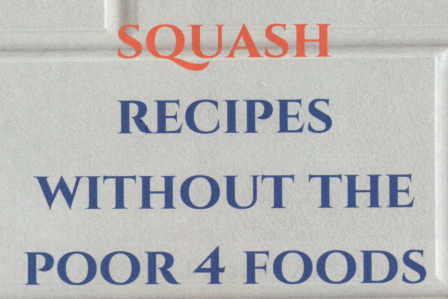

SQUASH
RECIPES
WITHOUT THE
POOR 4 FOODS

PEACE OVER PAIN

45 Minutes

Serves 2

BAKED SPAGHETTI SQUASH

Ingredients:

- 1 spaghetti squash
- 1 tbsp of ghee or butter
- Pink salt
- Pepper

Procedure:

- Preheat oven to 350F / 175C
- Cut spaghetti squash in half. Scoop out seeds (discard). Cut small piece to make sit flat on pan. Put in oven (no butter) cook for 25 minutes
- Turn down oven to 275 F / 135C. Place butter in cavity and bake for 20 minutes. Periodically coating in butter.
- Cook until tender and scoop the insides out, should look like spaghetti. Serve immediately or mix with a sauce.

15 Minutes

Serves 4

PEACE OVER PAIN

BUTTERNUT PUREE

Ingredients:

- 4 LB of butternut squash, scrubbed and left whole
- 4 oz of butter or ghee
- 1/2 cup of cream
- Pink salt
- Pepper

Procedure:

- Pierce the squash and place it in the roasting pan. Add enough water to create steam during the initial roasting time. Cover with a lid or foil if desired.
- Roast at 375 F / 19C until the squash is extremely tender, about an hour. To check for donees, piece with the kitchen fork or paring knife.
- Remove from the oven. As soon as the squash can be safely handles (it should still be hot), cut in half and remove the seeds.
- Scoop the flesh from the skin and puree it in a blender or food processor. If necessary, simmer the puree to reduce it.
- Add the butter, cream and seasoning to taste the salt and pepper. The puree is ready to use at once, or it may be properly cooled and held for later service.

25 Minutes

Serves 4

ZUCCHINI PARM

Ingredients:

- 2 zucchini
- 1/4 cup of parmesan cheese, grated
- 2 garlic cloves, minced
- 1 tbsp of butter or ghee
- 1 tsp of oregano
- 1/2 tsp of pink salt
- 1/4 tsp of pepper

Procedure:

- Preheat the oven to 300F / 150C. Line a baking sheet with parchment paper.
- Cut zucchini lengthwise into quarters and put in a bowl.
- Pour butter or ghee over zucchini and add minced garlic. With your hands, rub the garlic and butter all over the zucchini.
- Put the zucchini on the baking sheet in a single layer, skin side down.
- Sprinkle the zucchini wth salt, pepper, parmesan cheese and oregano.
- Put the zucchini in the oven on the top rack and bake for 15 minutes.
- Switch the oven to broil and bake for another 4 minutes, or until zucchini is golden brown.
- Serve warm. Optionally, you can sprinkle zucchini with exra parmesan cheese right before serving.

25 Minutes

Serves 4

PEACE OVER PAIN

ZUCCHINI BOATS

Ingredients:

- 4 medium zucchini, sliced into halves
- 1 cup of ricotta cheese
- 1 large egg
- 1 tbsp of chopped parsley
- 1 cup of shredded mozzarella
- 1/2 cup of parmesan cheese
- 8 oz of ground beef or ground turkey
- 4 tsp of ghee
- Pink salt
- 1-2 cups of oil free marinara sauce
- 1 tbsp of chopped basil

Procedure:

- Preheat the oven to 350F / 175C. Using a spoon, scoop centers from zucchini while leaving a 1/4 rim to create boats. Set aside.
- In a mixing bowl stir together ricotta cheese, egg and 1 tbsp of the parsley. Season lightly with salt and pepper. Stir in 1/2 cup of the mozzarella and parmesan cheese. Set aside.
- heat 2 tsp of ghee in a large non tick pan over medium heat.
- Crumble beef/turkey into pan, season with salt and paper and cook, stiring occasionally and breaking up beef when stiring, until browned (drain any extra fat)
- Stir in marinara sauce and 1 tbsp of the basil, remove from heat.

25 Minutes

Serves 4

ZUCCHINI BOATS

Procedure Continued...

- To assemble boats, brush both sides of the zucchini lightly with remaining 2 tsp of ghee and place in two baking pans. Divide cheese mixture among zucchini spooning about 1 tbsp into each, then spread cheese mixture into the even layer.
- Divide sauce among zucchini adding a few heaping spoonfuls to each. Cover baking dishes with foil and place in oven side by side and bake in preheated oven 30 minutes.
- Remove from oven, sprinkle tops with remaining 3/4 cup mozzarella, return to oven and bake until cheese has melted and zucchini is tender, about 5 minutes. Sprinkle tops with fresh basil and parsley and serve warm.

35 Minutes

Serves 4

PEACE OVER PAIN

CAJUN BUTTERNUT FRIES

Ingredients:

- 1 Lb of butternut squash, peeled, seeded and cut into thick fries
- 1 pinch of pink salt
- 1/4 tsp of black pepper
- 1/2 tsp of cajun seasoning
- 3 tbsp of butter

Procedure:

- Preheat oven to 325F / 160 C. Place squash on the prepared baking sheet. Sprinkle with salt, black pepper and cajun seasoning.
- Bake in the preheated oven until lightly browned and tender, 20 to 30 minutes or until tender, turning once.
- Once tender remove from oven, toss with butter in bowl and serve.

VEGGIE

RECIPES

WITHOUT THE

POOR 4 FOODS

PEACE
OVER
PAIN

35 Minutes

Serves 4

C

Ingredients:

- 1 Lb of asparagus
- 1 tbsp of ghee
- 1/2 tsp of pink salt
- 1 small garlic clove
- 1 lemon (zest and 1 tsp juice from half, plus slices from the other half)

Procedure:

- Preheat the oven to 350F/175C. Cut off the tough bottom ends of the asparagus. Add the asparagus stalks to a foil-lined baking sheet. Drizzle them with ghee and add the pink salt and a few grinds of black pepper.
- Add the zest of 1/2 lemon and mix with your hands. Thinly slice 4 lemon wheels from the lemon, then add them right on the tray.
- Bake 10 to 15 minutes, until tender when pierced by a fork at the thickest part. The timing will depend on the thickness of the asparagus spears. Toss with the 1 tsp lemon juice, then serve.

ROASTED ONIONS

Ingredients:

- 1 cup of water
- 1 cup of red wine vinegar
- 2 tbsp of brown sugar
- 1 tsp of fresh rosemary chopped
- 1/2 tsp of pink salt
- 1/4 tsp of black pepper
- Pinch of red pepper flakes (optional)
- 4 large white or yellow onions
- 4 tbsp of butter
- 1 tsp of fresh rosemary chopped

Procedure:

- Blend marinate ingredients in small bowl and pour into a baking dish that will hold all 8 onion halves. Use baking sheet depending on size of onion
- Trim the end of onions and cut horizontal (leaving skin on) and place wide side down in marinate. Marinate overnight covered in refrigerator.
- Preheat oven to 400F/200C. Flip the onion over in the marinate and lay on the flat bottom of each side. Top each onion with a 1/2 tablespoon of butter and remaining teaspoon of rosemary.
- Roast uncovered in oven for 1 hour or until golden brown. Remove from heat, spoon reduced sauce over and sprinkle with parsley or more fresh chopped rosemary. Remove outer skins before eating and serve.

35 Minutes

Serves 4

ROASTED BROCCOLI

Ingredients:

- 1 Lb of broccoli, stem on
- 3 tbs of ghee
- 1/2 tsp of pink salt
- Ground pepper
- 1 medium garlic clove
- 2 tbsp of lemon juice

Procedure:

- Preheat the oven to 350F / 175C. Line a baking sheet with parchment paper.
- Chop the broccoli into medium-sized florets, leaving a good amount of stem for a nice shape. Mix the broccoli florets with 2 tablespoons of ghee and the pink salt. Roast for 20-25 minutes, until tender and slightly browned.
- When the broccoli is done, remove the pan from the oven. Grate the garlic into the pan and add the remaining 1 tablespoon of ghee and the lemon juice. Use a spoon to gently toss it all together.

GARLIC CARROTS

Ingredients:

- 2 Lb of carrots, diagonally cut into about 2 to 3 inch pieces
- 5 tbsp of butter
- 4 garlic cloves, minced
- 1/4 tsp of pink salt
- 1/4 tsp of fresh ground pepper
- chopped fresh parsley

Procedure:

- Preheat oven to 300F / 150C
- Grease a baking sheet with butter, set aside
- Cut up the carrots and set aside
- Melt butter over medium-heat in a large pan
- Add garlic and cook for 3 minutes, or until lightly browned, stiring very frequently. Do not burn the garlic.
- Toss the carrots with the garlic butter either in the pan or pour the butter over them in a mixing bowl. Toss until well combined.
- Transfer carrots to previously prepared baking sheet.
- Arrange in one layer and bake for 22 to 30 minutes, or until carrots are tender.
- Remove from oven and transfer to a serving plate.
- Garnish with the parsley.

74

SAUTÉED VEGGIE MIX

Ingredients:

- 2 multi-colored bell peppers
- 1 medium red onion
- 1 large carrot
- 1 head broccoli, stem on
- 2 tbsp of ghee
- 1 tsp of pink salt
- Black pepper

Procedure:

- Thinly slice the peppers. Slice the onion. Cut the carrot into thin rounds. Cut the broccoli into small florets.
- Toss the veggies in a bowl with 1 tablespoon of ghee and the oregano, pink salt and plenty of black pepper.
- In a large pan, heat the remaining 1 tablespoon of ghee over medium high heat. Cook for 10 to 12 minutes until tender. Taste and add a few pinches of additional salt to taste.

20 Minutes

Serves 4

LAMB

RECIPES
WITHOUT THE
POOR 4 FOODS

PEACE OVER PAIN

25 Minutes

Serves 4

HERB CRUSTED RACK OF LAMB

Ingredients:

- 2 large racks of lamb, cut in half with 3 bones per serving
- Pink salt and pepper to taste
- 2 tbsp of ghee or cooking fat
- 4 slices of GF stale bread made into crumbs
- 7 tbsp of grated parmesan
- 1 sprig of parsley
- 1 sprig of thyme
- 1 sprig of rosemary
- 2 tbsp of dijon mustard (oil free)

Procedure:

- Preheat the oven to 400F/200C. Place lamb on cutting board fat side up. Lightly score the fat layer with a sharp knife. Generously sprinkle the lamb with salt and pepper. Mop up the excess seasoning with the rack of lamb, ensuring it's thoroughly coated.
- Heat some ghee in an oven safe pan. Set the lamb by holding each side in the ghee long enough to develop color (don't burn your hands). Brown the lamb
- Transfer the pan with the lamb into the oven and bake for 7-8 minutes. Prepare the crust while the lamb is cooking. **Continue on next page...**

HERB CRUSTED RACK OF LAMB

Procedure Continued...

- Crust - Place all of the ingredients for the crust except the mustard into a blender and pulse several times until it looks nice an green. Make sure you don't over do it with the ghee, just a little bit.
- Pour the mixture into the deep dish and set aside.
- Remove the lamb from oven and brush with mustard. Dip the lamb into the crust mixture coating it completely. Dip several times to ensure an even coating. Allow meat to rest. Place back in oven for 3-4 minutes when you're ready to serve.

25 Minutes

Serves 4

PEACE OVER PAIN

GARLIC LAMB CHOPS

Ingredients:

- 8 lamb loin chops
- 1 tbsp of pink salt
- 1 tbsp of black pepper
- 1 tbsp of thyme
- 3 tbsp of ghee
- 10 small garlic cloves, halved
- 3 tbsp of water
- 2 tbsp of lemon juice
- 2 tbsp of minced parsley

Procedure:

- Season the lamb with salt and pepper and sprinkle lightly with thyme. In a very large pan, heat the ghee until shimmering. Add the lamb chops and garlic and cook over moderately high heat until the chops are browned on the bottom, about 3 minutes. Turn the chops and garlic and cook until the chops are browned about 2 minutes longer for medium meat. Transfer the chops to plates, leaving the garlic in the pan.
- Add the water, lemon juice and parsley to the pan and cook, scraping up any browed bits stuck to the bottom, until sizzling about 1 minute. Pour the garlic and sauce over the lamb chops and serve immediately.

60 minutes

Serves 4

GARLIC CRUSTED RACK OF LAMB

Ingredients:

- 2 racks of lamb (2 Lb each)
- 1 bulb of garlic, cloves peeled
- 1/4 cup of rosemary leaves
- 1/4 cup of ghee
- Pink salt and ground pepper

Procedure:

- In a mini food processor, combine the garlic, rosemary and ghee and process until the garlic is finely chopped. Season the lamb racks with salt and pepper and rub the garlic-rosemary ghee all over them. Set the racks fat side up on a large rimmed baking sheet and let stand for 1 hour.
- Preheat the oven to 450C. Roast the lamb in the upper third of the oven for 15 minutes. Turn the racks and roast for 10 minutes longer for medium-rare meat. Transfer the racks to a carving board, stand them upright and let rest for 10 minutes.
- Carve the racks in between the rib bones and transfer to plate. Serve right away.

ROASTED LEG OF LAMB

Ingredients:

- 5 to 6 Lb trimmed bone in leg of lamb
- 4 garlic cloves, minced
- 1 tbsp of ghee
- 1 tbsp of rosemary
- 1 tbsp of thyme leaves
- 1 tbsp digon mustard
- 1 tbsp of pink salt
- 2 tsp of ground black pepper

Procedure:

- Preheat oven to 350F/175C
- Pat lamb dry with paper towels. Using a sharp knife, score the top side of the lamb by making shallow cuts all over.
- In a small bowl, combine garlic, ghee, rosemary, thyme, digon, salt and pepper
- Place lamb, fat side up, on a rack in the prepared roasting pan. Spread garlic mixture evenly over lamb, rubbing in throughly into the scored cuts.
- Place into oven and roast until it reaches an internal temperature of 135F /57C for medium, about 1 hour 30 minutes to 1 hour 45 minutes, or until desired doneness. Let rest 15 minutes before slicing.

60 Minutes

Serves 8

PEACE OVER PAIN

FENNEL-RUBBED LEG OF LAMB W/ SALSA VERDE

Ingredients:

- 4 to 5 Lb of boneless leg of lamb
- 2 tbsp of pink salt
- 3 tbsp of ground pepper
- 4 tsp of crushed red pepper flakes
- 4 garlic cloves, finely grated
- 3 tbsp of ghee
- 2 Lb of small or medium carrots
- 1/2 cup of chopped parsley
- 1/4 cup of chopped chives
- 2 tbs of lemon juice

Procedure:

- Season lamb generously with salt and pepper; let it sit out at room temperature while you prepare the rub.
- Using a spice mill or mortar and pestle, coarsely grind fennel seeds and red pepper flakes. Transfer to a small bowl and mix in garlic and 3 tbsp ghee. Evenly rub lamb all over with spice mixture, making sure to work it into every nook and cranny.
- Preheat oven to 300F. Heat the ghee in a large heavy pan over medium. As soon as ghee is hot add lamb to pan and cook, carefully pouring off fat as needed into a small bowl, until golden brown all over, 3-5 minutes per side. The goal is to cook out some of the excess fat while you brown the meat, so it's important to maintain a moderate heat to keep the meat from getting dark before the fat can melt out. **Continue on next page...**

60 Minutes

Serves 8

PEACE OVER PAIN

FENNEL-RUBBED LEG OF LAMB W/ SALSA VERDE

Procedure Continued...

- Trim tops of carrots and set aside for making salsa verde. Scrub carrots, pat dry and scatter along the outer edges of a large rimmed baking sheet. Place seared lamb in the center. Pour reserved fat and any fat still in pan over carrots, season with salt and paper and toss to coat.

- Roast lamb and carrots until an instant read thermometer inserted into the center of leg registers 135 F for medium-rare 75-90 minutes. Transfer lamb to a cutting board and tent with foil; let rest 20 minutes. Leave oven on.

- While the lamb is resting, transfer carrots to a plater, then carefully pour any juices from the baking sheet into a small bowl (you have about 1/4 cup; discard remaining tops. Place in a small bowl and mix in parsley, chives, lemon juice, pan juices and 2 tbsp ghee. Season with salt and pepper and more lemon juice if needed.

- Remove twine from lamb and slice about 1/2 thick (but you can really go as thick or thin as you would like). Arrange on a platter and serve with warm roasted carrots and salsa verde alongside.

SOUP

RECIPES

WITHOUT THE

POOR 4 FOODS

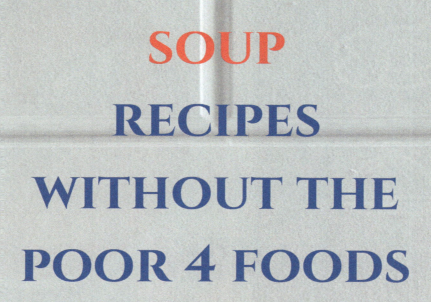

PEACE
OVER
PAIN

15 Minutes

Makes 1 Cup

PEACE OVER PAIN

TOMATO SOUP

Ingredients:

- 4 tbsp of ghee
- 1/2 large onion, cut into large wedges
- 28 oz of canned tomatoes, whole peeled or crushed. For fresh tomatoes use 4 cups peeled and crushed
- 1 cup of water or chicken stock
- 1/2 tsp of pink salt

Procedure:

- Melt ghee over medium heat in a large pot or pan
- Add onion wedges, water, tomatoes and 1/2 teaspoon of salt. Bring to a simmer. Cook, uncovered, for about 40 minutes. Stir occasionally and add additional salt as needed.
- Blend the soup and then season to taste. The soup doesn't need to be ultra smooth, some texture is good.

20 Minutes

Serves 4

PEACE OVER PAIN

CHICKEN NOODLE SOUP

Ingredients:

- 2 tbsp of ghee
- 1 cup of sweet onion, finely chopped
- 1 cup of carrots, cut into small pieces
- 1/2 cup of celery cut into small pieces
- 2 garlic cloves, crushed
- 1 Lb of chicken breast cut into small pieces
- 1 tsp of pink salt
- 1/2 tsp of dried sage
- 1/2 tsp of dried thyme
- 3 to 4 cups of chicken broth
- 3 cups of water
- 2 cups of milk or cream
- 6 oz of GF pasta (optional

Procedure:

- In a large pot add ghee, onion, carrots and celery.
- Saute' over medium until onions are translucent.
- Add garlic and continue cooking over medium heat until ingredients are aromatic, stirring occasionally.
- Cut chicken into cubes and cook for 4-5 minutes, or until chicken is almost cooked through.
- Add salt, pepper, sage, thyme, chicken broth, water and milk. Increase heat to high and bring soup to a boil.
- Once soup is boiling, add pasta and cook for 7-10 minutes, or until noodles are cooked through.
- Salt to taste.

86

15 Minutes

Serves 4

CREAM OF MUSHROOM

Ingredients:

- 5 cups of fresh mushrooms, sliced
- 1 cups of chicken broth
- 1/2 cup of onion, chopped
- 1/8 tsp of dried thyme
- 3 tbsp of ghee
- 3 tbsp of GF all purpose flour
- 1/4 tsp of pink salt
- 1/4 tsp of black pepper
- 1 cup of milk or cream
- 1 tbsp of sherry

Procedure:

- In a large heavy pan, cook mushrooms in the broth with onion and thyme until tender, about 10 to 15 minutes.
- In blender, or food processor, puree the mixture, leaving some chunks of vegetable in it. Set aside.
- In the pan, melt the ghee, whisk in the flour until smooth. Add the salt, pepper, milk or cream and vegetable puree. Stirring constantly, bring soup to a boil and cook until thickened. Adjust seasonings to taste and add sherry.

POTATO SOUP

Ingredients:

- 3 cups of yukon gold potatoes peeled and diced
- 1/2 cup of green onion diced
- 1/2 cup of celery diced
- 32 oz of chicken stock or veggie broth
- 2 cups of milk
- 1 cup of sour cream or greek yogurt
- 3 tbsp of GF all purpose flour
- Preservative free turkey bacon
- Shredded cheese

Procedure:

- Bring first four ingredients to a boil, then reduce to simmer. Cover and cook until vegetables are tender, about 15 minutes. Do not overcook.
- Add 1 cup of milk to the pot. In a bowl, stir together 2 tablespoons of flour, 1 cup of milk and 1 cup of sour cream/yogurt until blended. Add mixture to the pot. Cook until thickened, stirring frequently.
- Add bacon or ham if desired. top with shredded cheese.

15 Minutes

Makes 1 Cup

DAL SOUP

Ingredients:

- 2 tbsp of ghee
- 1 tbsp of garlic, chopped
- 1 tsp of turmeric
- 1 tbsp of garam masala
- Pinch of pink salt
- 1 cup of tomatoes, chopped
- 1 cup of brown lentils
- 6 cups of water
- Cilantro sprigs

Procedure:

- Heat the ghee in a pan over medium heat until it begins to get hot. Add garlic and spices and cook for 20 seconds.
- Add tomatoes, lentils and water, cover and bring to a boil. Turn heat to low and simmer until the lentils are tender, about 25 to 30 minutes.
- Serve in bowl and garnish with fresh cilantro sprigs.

DIP

RECIPES WITHOUT THE POOR 4 FOODS

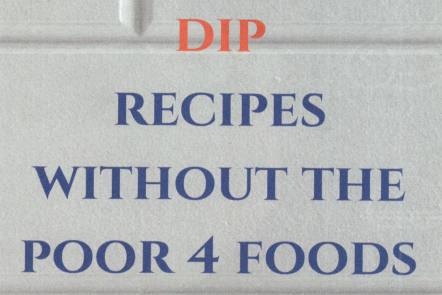

15 Minutes

Makes 1-1/2 Cups

PEACE OVER PAIN

ONION DIP

Ingredients:

- 1 Lb of mixed onions (sweet, yellow, red)
- 4 garlic cloves, unpeeled
- 1/4 cup of ghee
- 1 whole greek yogurt
- 2 tsp of lemon juice
- Pink salt to taste
- Ground black pepper to taste

Procedure:

- Preheat oven to 350F / 175C. peel and trim ends off onions. Cut onions in half. Place halves, cut side down on cutting board, then thinly slice.
- Line a rimmed baking sheet with parchment paper. In a mixing bowl, toss onion and 4 garlic cloves with 1/4 cup of ghee and 2 tbsp water until evenly coated. Season with salt and toss again until well coated. Mount onions and garlic together in center of sheet pan rather than spreading them out.
- Bake, tossing and stirring onions every 10 minutes, until all onions are golden brown and softened, 40-50 minutes total. Some onions will brown more than others but that's ok. Let it cool.
- Transfer onions and garlic to a cutting board and squeeze out garlic cloves from peel. Using the flat side of knife, small garlic cloves to a paste. Transfer to a medium bowl.
- Finely chop caramelized onions and transfer to a bowl with garlic
- Add 1 cup of yogurt and 2 tsp lemon juice; season with salt and pepper. Stir to combine. Sprinkle dip with cayenne pepper.

15 Minutes

Makes 1 Cup

PEACE OVER PAIN

RANCH DIP

Ingredients:

- 1/2 cup of sour cream or greek yogurt
- 4 tbsp of heavy cream or buttermilk
- 2 tbsp of white wine vinegar
- 2 tsp of dry dill weed or 2 tbsp of chopped fresh dill
- 1 tsp of garlic, granulated
- Pink salt and black pepper

Procedure:

- Stir all ingredients together in a bowl
- Cover and chill for 30 minutes in a refrigerator to let all the flavors mingle

15 Minutes

Makes 1 Cup

TACO DIP

Ingredients:

- 16 oz of sour cream or greek yogurt
- 1 oz of packaged taco seasoning (oil free) or make your own with 1 tbsp of chili powder, 1/4 tsp of garlic powder, 1/4 tsp of onion powder, 1/4 tsp of crushed red pepper flakes, 1/4 tsp of dried oregano, 1/2 tsp of paprika, 1 tsp of ground cumin, 1 tsp of pink salt, 1 tsp of black pepper

Procedure:

- Mix together well
- Let sit in a fridge at least 1 hour before serving.

1 hour

Makes 1 Cup

PEACE OVER PAIN

GUACAMOLE

Ingredients:

- 3 avocados, peeled & pitted (no brown or black spots)
- 1/2 cup of onions, diced
- 2 roma plum tomatoes, diced
- 1 tsp of garlic, minced
- 1 tbsp of lime or lemon juice
- 3 tbsp of cilantro, chopped
- 1 tsp of pink salt

Procedure:

- In a medium bowl, mash together the avocados, lime juice and salt.
- Mix in onion, cilantro, tomatoes and garlic. Stir in cayenne pepper. Refrigerate 1 hour for best flavor or serve immediately.

15 Minutes

Makes 1 Cup

PEACE OVER PAIN

HUMMUS

Ingredients:

- 1 can or box of chickpeas (rinsed and drained). If using dry chickpeas, soak 8-10 hours.
- 2 cloves of garlic, chopped
- 2 to 3 tbsp of lemon juice
- 3 tbsp of water or stock

Procedure:

- Using a food processor, blend all the ingredients into a thick paste, using a small amount of water as necessary to achieve desired consistency.
- Serve chilled or at room temp. Can store in refrigerator up to one month.

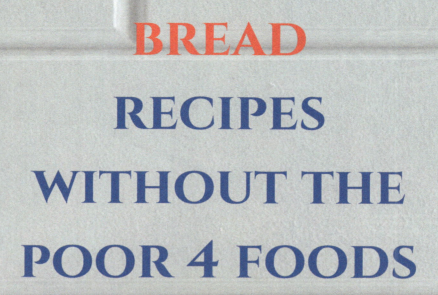

BREAD

RECIPES WITHOUT THE POOR 4 FOODS

PEACE OVER PAIN

A few hours

Makes 1 Loaf

PEACE OVER PAIN

CLASSIC BREAD

Ingredients:

- 1 cup of warm water
- 2 tbsp of honey
- 2 tsp of dry active yeast
- 1 cup of white rice flour
- 3/4 cup of tapioca starch
- 1/2 cup of millet or almond flour
- 1/4 cup of ground flaxseed
- 2 tsp of xanthan gum or chia seeds
- 1 tsp of baking powder
- 1 tsp of pink salt
- 1/4 cup of ghee
- 3 eggs whites
- 1 tsp of apple cider vinegar

Procedure:

- Line a metal loaf pan with parchment paper and grease with ghee, set it aside.
- Add the honey and yeast to your warm water and stir; set it aside for 5-10 minutes but no longer.
- In the bowl of a stand mixer fitted with the paddle attachment, add the flours, flax seed meal, xanthan gum, baking powder, and salt. Turn your mixer to low and mix just until combined.
- With the mixer still going, add the clarified butter, egg whites, vinegar and proofed yeast mixture.
- Turn the mixer to a medium speed and mix for an additional 2 minutes. The dough will be thick and sticky. Using a rubber spatula, add the dough to your prepared loaf pan making sure to fill in the corners of the pan and level the top. Wet your fingers and smooth the top.

Continue on next page

A few hours

Makes 1 Loaf

CLASSIC BREAD

Procedure Continued...

- Cover the dough with ghee and wrap with the plastic wrap and allow it to rise in a warm place for 45 to 60 minutes or until it has risen slightly above the loaf pan.
- When the dough is near the top of the pan, preheat your oven to 350F / 175C.
- Remove the plastic wrap and bake for 60-65 minutes. Half way through baking, cover the bread loaf with a piece of foil to keep it from over browning.
- Remove the loaf from the oven and let cool completely before slicing.
- Slice the entire loaf and store in a container at room temperature for up to 4 days or in the freezer for up to a month.

CHEESE BREAD

Ingredients:

- 1 cup of tapicoa flour
- 1 egg
- 1/4 cup of ghee
- 2/3 cup of milk
- 1/2 cup of any white cheese, grated
- 1/2 tsp of pink salt

Procedure:

- Preheat oven to 325f / 160C. Grease a standard muffin pan with ghee.
- Combine all ingredients in a blender. Pulse until ingredient are completely combined, stopping to scrape down the sides of the blender with a spatula as needed.
- Pour batter into muffins tins, filling a little over halfway. Bake for about 20 minutes, until the tops of the buns are lightly browned.
- Cool for 2 minutes before removing from the pan. Serve immediately.

A few hours

Makes 1 Loaf

PEACE OVER PAIN

ARTISAN BREAD

Ingredients:

- 3 1/2 cups Gluten-Free All Purpose Blend
- 3 1/2 cups 100% Whole-Grain Gluten-Free Flour
- 1 tablespoon granulated yeast
- 1 1/4 tablespoons kosher salt
- 2 tablespoons raw cane sugar
- 4 3/4 cups lukewarm water, 100 F or below
- 1 tablespoon poppy seeds
- 1 tablespoon raw hemp seeds
- cornmeal or parchment paper for the pizza peel

Procedure:

- Whisk together the flours, seeds, yeast, salt and sugar in a 5-to-6 quart bowl, or a 5 quart dutch oven
- Add the water and mix with a spoon. Cover (not airtight), and allow to rest at room temperature until the dough rises, approximately 2 hours. Don't be surprised that it doesn't rise much. This is normal.
- The dough can be used immediately after the initial rise, though it is easier to handle when cold.
- Refrigerate it in a lidded (not airtight) container and use over the next 10 days. Or freeze for up to 4 weeks in 1-pound portions and thaw in the refrigerator overnight before using.

A few hours

Makes 6 Pieces

PEACE OVER PAIN

INDIAN NAAN BREAD

Ingredients:

- 1/4 cup of plain coconut yogurt
- 1/2 cup of coconut milk (canned if needed)
- 1 tsp of ghee
- 2 tsp of baking powder
- 1/2 tsp of pink salt
- 2 small cloves of garlic, minced
- 1/2 cup of coconut flour
- 1/2 cup of arrowroot starch
- 1/2 cup of potato or tapioca starch
- 1/4 cup of GF all purpose flour

Procedure:

- In a medium mixing bowl add coconut yogurt, coconut milk, ghee, baking powder, salt, garlic and whisk. The mixture will likely fluff up and foam if your yogurt has active cultures.
- Next add coconut flour, arrowroot starch and potato starch and stir with a wooden spoon to combine. It should form a dough that is moist and malleable, doesn't stick to your hands and also doesn't crack easily when rolled. Add more potato starch as needed if to sticky. Add more light coconut milk as needed if it's too dry.
- Generously sprinkle gluten free flour on a clean surface and place 1 ball of dough (3 tbsp in size) in the center. Generously dust the top of the dough with GF flour. Use a rolling pin to roll into a thin oval shape, about 1/4 thick. **Continue on next page**

A few hours

Makes 6 Pieces

INDIAN NAAN BREAD

Procedure Continued...

- Heat a pan over medium high heat. Heat up ghee then use a spatula to carefully transfer the dough to the pan.
- Cook for 3-4 minutes or until the underside is golden brown. Bubbles may form while it's cooking - that's normal and good. Flip carefully and cook for another 2-3 minutes. Lower heat as needed to ensure it doesn't burn. It's done when both sides are golden brown.
- Repeat this process until all naan dough is used.
- Garnish with minced garlic and or some parsley if desired. Store leftovers covered in the refrigerator up to 2-3 days.

FRENCH BAGUETTE

Ingredients:

- 2 cups of white rice flour
- 1 cup of tapioca flour
- 3 tsp of xanthan gum
- 1 tsp of pink salt
- 1 egg
- 2 tbsp of honey
- 1 cup of lukewarm water
- 2 tbsp of fast rise yeast
- 2 tbsp of ghee
- 3 egg whites, beaten slightly
- 1 tsp of vinegar

Procedure:

- In the bowl of a heavy duty mixer, place flours, xanthan gum, salt, and egg replacer (if used). Blend with mixer on low.
- In a small bowl dissolve the sugar in the water and add yeast.
- Wait until the mixture foams slightly, then blend into the dry ingredients.
- Add the butter, egg whites and vinegar. Beat on high for 3 minutes.
- To form loaves, spoon dough onto greased and cornmeal-dusted cookie sheets in two long french loaf shapes or spoon into special french bread pans.
- Slash diagonally every few inches. If desired, brush with melted ghee.
- Cover the dough and let rise in a warm place until doubled in bulk, 20 to 25 minutes.
- Preheat oven to 325F / 160C and bake for 50-60 minutes.
- Remove from pan to cool.

PIZZA CRUST

RECIPES WITHOUT THE POOR 4 FOODS

20 Minutes

12 inch crust

PEACE OVER PAIN

BASIC PIZZA CRUST

Ingredients:

- 3 cups of GF flour
- 1 cup of warm water
- 1 tbsp of yeast (dry, fresh)
- 2 tbsp of sugar
- 1 tsp of pink salt

Procedure:

- Mix warm water, sugar and yeast together, let that sit for 5 minutes.
- Add flour and salt to the water, sugar and yeast. Mix this until smooth and let it rise for 10 minutes. Use mixer for the dough if you have one.
- Prepare the dough for what you will be making and let rest for another 10 minutes before pouring into the oven.
- Bake at 400F / 200C for 15-20 minutes.
- If making a pizza, you can cut the dough recipe in half and make a thinner crust pizza and bread twists.

SPINACH PIZZA CRUST

20 Minutes

12 inch crust

Ingredients:

- 2 cups of spinach
- 1 egg
- 1/2 cup of mozzarella cheese, shredded
- 1 tsp of basil
- 1/2 tsp of oregano

Procedure:

- Preheat oven to 425F / 220C
- Blend spinach and mozzarella in a food processor
- Add egg and blend.
- Spread on parchment paper and bake for 15 minutes. Edges should brown.
- Add your favorite sauce and toppings and broil until cheese melts.

106

60 Minutes

12 inch crust

PEACE OVER PAIN

CAULIFLOWER PIZZA CRUST

Ingredients:

- 2 LB of large head of cauliflower or 2 LBs of store bought cauliflower rice
- 1 large egg
- 1 tsp of italian seasoning or dried oregano/basil
- 1/8 tsp of pink salt
- 1/4 tsp black pepper
- 1/2 cup of parmesan or mozzarella cheese

Procedure:

- Preheat oven to 375F / 190C and line baking sheet with unbleached parchment paper or silicon mat.
- Make "rice" - Rice cauliflower, remove the outer leaves, separate into florets and chop into small pieces. Process in a food processor in 2 batches, until "rice" texture forms (skip if using store-bought).
- Transfer cauliflower rice on a prepared baking sheet and bake for 15 minutes. Remove cooked cauliflower rice from the oven, transfer to a large bowl lined with a double/triple layered cheesecloth or linen towel, and let cool for 15 minutes or until safe to touch.
- Squeeze the liquid out of the ball (cauliflower inside the cheesecloth) as hard as you can.
- Make dough: Increase oven temperature to 350F / 175C. In a medium mixing bowl whisk the egg with dried herbs, salt and pepper. Add cheese and squeezed cauliflower; mix very well with spatula until combined. **Continue on next page**

60 Minutes

12 inch crust

CAULIFLOWER PIZZA CRUST

Procedure Continue:

- Line same baking sheet with new parchment paper or silicone mat (just make sure to scrape off any bits of cauliflower) and spread ghee on the pan. Transfer cauliflower pizza dough in the middle and flatten with your hands until thin pizza crust forms.
- Bake crust first: Bake for 20 minutes and carefully flip with spatula and bake for a few more minutes.
- Bake pizza with toppings: Top cauliflower pizza base with your favorite toppings and bake again until cheese is golden brown.
- Cut into 8 slices and serve.
- Refrigerate leftover covers for up 2 days. Freeze for up to 3 months. Thaw completely before baking with toppings.

SAUCE

RECIPES

WITHOUT THE

POOR 4 FOODS

MARINARA SAUCE

Ingredients:

- 2 cans of crushed tomatoes
- 2 tbsp of dried oregano
- 2 tbsp of dried basil
- 2 tsp of onion powder
- 1 tsp of garlic powder
- 1/4 red pepper flakes
- 2 tbsp of maple syrup or honey
- Pink salt

Procedure:

- Place all ingredients in a large pot and simmer over medium to medium high heat for 2-3 minutes.
- Reduce heat to low and cook for another 5-6 minutes, stirring occasionally.
- Serve over your favorite gluten free pasta or gluten free pizza crust.

10 Minutes

Makes 1 cups

PEACE OVER PAIN

KETCHUP

Ingredients:

- 6 oz of tomato paste
- 2 tbsp of apple cider vinegar
- 1 tbsp of water
- 2 tbsp of sugar
- 1/2 tsp of pink salt
- 1/4 tsp of onion powder
- 1/4 tsp of garlic powder
- 1/4 tsp of mustard powder
- Pinch of ground cinnamon, ground all spice, ground cloves, cayenne pepper, to taste

Procedure:

- Whisk together all ingredients in a medium saucepan until smooth.
- Add extra water 1 tablespoon at a time if necessary until you have the desired consistency. Most people like it thin.
- Cook on medium heat until ketchup is hot and bubbles begin to break at the surface. Stir constantly for 1-2 minutes and remove from the heat.
- Allow ketchup to cool completely before placing in airtight container.
- Store in airtight container for 1-2 months in refrigerator.

10 Minutes

Makes 1 cups

PEACE OVER PAIN

MUSTARD

Ingredients:

- 1 cup of cold water
- 3/4 cups of yellow dried mustard
- 3/4 tsp of pink salt
- 1/2 tsp of ground turmeric
- 1 tsp of garlic puree or 1/8 tsp of garlic powder
- 1/8 tsp of paprika
- 1/2 cup of apple cider vinegar

Procedure:

- Add all ingredients in a pot, whisk until smooth.
- Cook on a medium-low or low heat, until thickens to a paste.
- Whisk in vinegar and cook until desired consistency. Let mustard cool to a room temp before using or storing up to 3 months in refrigerator. Mustard will taste strongest after cooking and let it mellow out in the fridge.

10 Minutes

Makes 2 cups

BBQ SAUCE

Ingredients:

- 2 cups of sugar-free / organic ketchup
- 1/2 cup of apple cider vinegar
- 4 tbsp of brown sugar
- 2 tbsp of honey
- 1 tbsp of lemon juice
- 1 tsp of house seasoning
- 1/4 tsp of hot sauce

Procedure:

- Whisk together all ingredients in a medium saucepan situated over medium heat. Allow to come to a bubble and then reduce the heat to low. Allow to simmer until thickened, about 10 minutes.
- Serve immediately or allow to cool slightly and store in an airtight container in the refrigerator for up to a week.

30 Minutes

Makes 2 cups

PEACE OVER PAIN

HOT SAUCE

Ingredients:

- 18 cayenne peppers, ends and stems removed
- 1 cup of apple cider vinegar
- 3 tsp of garlic, minced
- 1 tsp of pink salt
- 1 tsp of garlic powder

Procedure:

- There are two different ways to prepare this sauce. You can use fresh cayenne peppers or you can use cayenne peppers from your garden that you have canned.
- If you're using fresh cayenne peppers, simply remove the ends and measure all of the ingredients into a small saucepan.
- Heat over medium heat until boiling.
- Reduce the heat slightly, but so the mixture continues to boil.
- simmer about 20-25 minutes.
- Remove the mixture from heat, carefully pour it into a blender and puree until thick and smooth.
- Transfer the mixture back into the pan and simmer another 15 minutes.
- In a blender add 18 peppers, 1 cup of vinegar, garlic, salt and garlic powder.
- Cover and puree until smooth.
- Transfer to a saucepan and bring to a boil
- Reduce heat and simmer to 20 minutes.

DESSERT

RECIPES
WITHOUT THE
POOR 4 FOODS

6 Hours

Serves 4

VANILLA ICE CREAM

Ingredients:

- 2 cups of heavy whipping cream
- 14 oz can of sweetened condensed milk
- 1 tsp of pure vanilla extract

Procedure:

- In a large bowl, use a hand mixer or a stand mixer to whip the cream until stiff peaks occur, be careful not to very whip. The cream will be done when you pull the beaters out and the cream stands at attention.
- In another large bowl, whisk the vanilla into the sweetened condensed milk. Gently fold in the whipped cream with a spatula, slowly incorporating the two mixtures together so it stays light and saerated.
- If making individual flavors, scoop the cream mixture into smaller bowls and gently fold in your desired fruit mix-ins or if making just vanilla, mix the ingredients directly into the cream mixture.
- Transfer the mixture to an insulated tub or paper containers and freeze for 4-6 hours.

10 minutes

Serves 4

CHOCOLATE MOUSSE

Ingredients:

- 1 cups of heavy whipping cream
- 4 tbsp of un-sweetened cocoa powder, sifted
- 4 tbsp of powdered sweetener
- 1 tsp of vanilla extract
- 1/4 tsp of pink salt

Procedure:

- Whisk the cream to stiff peaks using mixer or by hand, it will take some time.
- Add in the cocoa powder, sweetener, vanilla and salt and whisk until all ingredients are just combined.
- Top with fruits of your choice.

15 minutes

Makes 12-18

CHEESECAKE FLUFF

Ingredients:

- 1 cup of heavy whipping cream
- 8 oz of cream cheese, softened
- Zest of 1 lemon
- 1 cup of granular sweetener

Procedure:

- Add the heavy cream to a stand mixer and whisk until stiff peaks are formed. You can also use a hand mixer or whip by hand with a whisk.
- Remove the whipped cream to a separate bowl and set aside.
- Add the softened cream cheese, zest and sweetener to the stand mixer bowl and beat until smooth.
- Pour the whipped cream into the stand mixer bowl with the cream cheese. Stir gently with a spatula until it is halfway incorporated. Use the stand mixer to finish whipping until smooth.
- Serve with your favorite fruit toppings.

15 Minutes

Serves 10

BUTTER COOKIE FAT BOMBS

Ingredients:

- 1 cup of almond flour
- 2 tbsp of honey
- 3 tbsp of ghee, melted
- 1 tsp of vanilla extract
- Pinch of pink salt

Procedure:

- Combine all ingredients in a small bowl. The mixture should be wet enough to stick together. Scoop out 1 tbsp of the mixture at a time and roll into a ball. The balls should be 1-1/4 inch in diameter.
- Refrigerate for 1 hour before serving.

RICE KRISPY SQUARES

Ingredients:

- 8 cups of GF rice cereal
- 2 oz of ghee
- 16 oz of mini GF grass-fed/organic marshmallows, divided
- 1 tsp of pure vanilla extract
- 1/4 tsp of pink salt

Procedure:

- Grease a baking sheet with ghee. Set aside 1-2 cups of the mini marshmallows.
- In a large pot, melt the ghee over low heat. Once the ghee is melted, start to whisk constantly. First the ghee will begin to foam, then after a couple of minutes it will begin to brown on the bottom of the saucepan.
- Add all but the reserved cup of marshmallows and cook on low, stirring constantly until mostly melted, a few small lumps here and there are fine.
- Remove from the heat and add the vanilla and salt and stir to combine.
- Add the cereal and stir 2-3 times then add the reserved marshmallows and continue to stir until the cereal is coated. A few chunks of marshmallows will remain.
- Scrape the mixture into the prepared pan and using lightly greased or barely wet hands, lightly press the mixture into the pan. Let cool for at least 20 minutes before slicing.

25 Minutes

Makes 12 Squares

PRESSURE COOKER
RECIPES WITHOUT
THE POOR 4 FOODS

50 Minutes

Serves 4

SMOKED RIBS

Ingredients:

- 2 tbsp salt
- 2 tbsp brown sugar
- 1 tsp black pepper ground
- 1 tsp garlic powder
- 1 tsp onion powder
- 1 tsp chili powder
- 1 tsp red bell pepper crushed
- 2 lb pork ribs
- ¼ tsp liquid smoke
- 1 cup barbecue sauce

Procedure:

- Combine the first 7 ingredients and mix to make a rub. Set aside.
- Remove the membrane from the back of the ribs by loosening one end with a knife and grasping it with a paper towel and pulling.
- Apply the rub to both sides of the ribs and place in a ring inside the pressure cooker pot.
- Close and lock the pressure cooker lid. Make sure the steam release handle is turned to sealing. Press Pressure Cook, pressure level High, and set the time to 30 Minutes. Then press Cancel and let the pressure release on its own.
- Preheat the oven to 395°F (200°C).
- Transfer ribs to the roaster and brush with your favorite BBQ sauce.
- Bake for 10 to 15 Minutes, watching to make sure the ribs don't burn.

40 Minutes

Serves 2

PEACE OVER PAIN

BLACK BEAN STEW

Ingredients:

- 3 tbsp of ghee
- ¼ tsp cumin
- ⅛ tsp pepper
- ⅛ tsp cinnamon
- Salt to taste
- 1 garlic clove finely minced
- 1 green onion finely chopped
- ½ cup zucchini diced
- 10 cherry tomatoes cut in half
- 1 cup black beans not soaked
- 2 cups vegetable or bone broth or water

Procedure:

- Add ghee, seasonings, vegetables, and beans to the pressure cooker.
- Press Saute. Set time to 2 Minutes.
- Stir with wooden spoon until time is up. Then add the broth or water. Stir.
- Close and lock the pressure cooker lid. Make sure the steam release handle is turned to Sealing. Press Pressure Cook, then set time to 30 Minutes.
- When done cooking, press Cancel and turn the steam release handle to Venting.
- Remove the lid from the pressure cooker. You can serve immediately or let it cool, store in a glass storage container, and refrigerate.

GARLIC HONEY CHICKEN

Ingredients:

- 1.3 kg whole chicken
- 1 tsp sea salt
- 3 garlic clove
- 2 bay leaf
- 3 tbsp Garlic butter melted
- ½ tbsp miso
- 1 tbsp honey
- 80 ml plain yogurt
- 2 tbsp oil free mayonnaise
- 5 g fresh basil leaves
- 4 g fresh chives
- ¼ clove garlic grated
- Water as needed
- Salt & pepper as needed

Procedure:

- Place the chicken on a trivet, sprinkle over the salt and cover completely in water, making sure not to exceed the maximum volume line.
- Add the whole, unshelled garlic cloves, and bay leaves to the water. Secure the pressure cooker.
- Pressure Cook on High for 0 Minutes. The food is going to be cooked while the pot is coming to pressure. When the time is up, allow for 19 Minutes natural release, then carefully quick-release the rest of the pressure.
- While the chicken cooks, make your green goddess sauce, by blending together yogurt, mayonnaise, basil, chives and garlic until the sauce is nice and smooth. Season to taste with salt and pepper. Set aside.
- Once the chicken has cooked, remove it from the cooking liquid and set aside. Reserve the broth for another use, like our super comforting and delicious chicken noodle soup. Save the garlic for the basting sauce.
- Clean and dry the inner pot. **Continued on next page**

45 Minutes

Serves 4

PEACE OVER PAIN

GARLIC HONEY CHICKEN

Procedure Continued...

- Squeeze the garlic out of their cloves, and add to a bowl along with the miso, honey, and garlic butter. Stir to combine.

- Place the chicken back into your cleaned pot, on the trivet. Brush over the miso honey sauce and place the air frying lid on your pressure cooker pot.

- Select Air Fry, set the temperature to 195°C / 385°F and the timer to 9 Minutes. Cook the chicken, basting a few more times, until golden brown. Add more time as needed until the chicken is browned to your liking.

- Once cooked, carve and serve immediately alongside your remaining miso sauce and green goddess sauce.

30 Minutes

Serves 6

LOADED BAKED POTATO SOUP

Ingredients:

- 4 slices of turkey bacon
- 4 cups of Chicken Broth
- 3 LB of yukon gold potato
- 1 tsp of salt
- 1/2 tsp of black pepper
- 4 oz of cream cheese
- 2 cups of half n half
- 1 cup of shredded mozzarella cheese
- 2 green onion

Procedure:

- Heat the inner pot - saute' on normal/medium
- Then add bacon to the inner pot and cook until crispy - 4 minutes
- Drain bacon fat, place cooked bacon in between two paper towels and set aside
- Pour chicken broth into the inner pot and deglaze with a wooden spoon
- Add potatoes, salt and pepper to the inner pot
- Pressure cook on high for 10 minutes. When the time is up, carefully quick release the pressure
- Blend with stick blender until slightly chunky
- Set cooker to saute on normal/medium again
- Whist cream cheese and half and half to the inner pot
- Cook while stiring occasionally - 10 minutes
- Mix in half of the cooked bacon
- Serve topped with remaining bacon, garnish with cheese and onions.

15 Minutes

Serves 2

Spicy Eggplant Stew

Ingredients:

- 2 tbsp of ghee
- 1 garlic finely minced
- 1 tsp cinnamon powder
- ¼ tsp white pepper
- ¼ tsp finely chopped cacho cabra chili pepper
- ½ white onion finely diced
- ½ eggplant diced
- 8 mushrooms
- ½ red bell pepper finely diced
- 1 tomato finely diced
- ¾ cup tomato sauce
- ½ cup bone broth or water
- salt to taste

Procedure:

- Place the stainless steel inner pot inside the pressure cooker. Press Saute. Set time to 4 Minutes. Add the ghee, seasonings, onion, and eggplant to the pressure cooker pot. Stir from time to time until Sauté ends.
- Add the rest of the vegetables, tomato sauce, and bone broth or water. Stir.
- Close and lock the pressure cooker lid. Make sure the steam release handle is turned to Sealing. Press Pressure Cook, pressure level High, and set time to 8 Minutes.
- When done cooking, press Cancel and turn the steam release handle to Venting.
- Open pot lid and serve. You can serve it with meat or go vegetarian with basmati rice. Both make a perfect combination.

AJIACO STEW

Ingredients:

- 1 chicken breast
- 1 Ear of corn cut in 4
- 4 criclla potatoes peeled and cut
- 2 potatoes peeled and cut
- 2 green onions
- Guascas herbs
- cilantro
- Whole garlic cloves
- 1 cup Water
- To serve:
- Sliced avocado

Procedure:

- Insert the stainless steel inner pot into the pressure cooker and add the chicken breast, corn on the cob, criolla potatoes, green onion, guascas herb, cilantro, whole garlic and water.
- Close and lock the pressure cooker lid Make sure the steam release handle is turned to Sealing. Press Soup/Broth and set time to 25 Minutes.
- Once the time is up, press Cancel and turn the steam release handle to Venting.
- Remove from pressure cooker, and serve with avocado slices.

128

40 Minutes

Serves 4

GREEK CHICKEN
W/ LEMON POTATOES

Ingredients:

- 4 bone-in beef scraps skin-on chicken thighs
- 2 lemons juiced and zested
- 3 tbsp ghee
- 2 tsp salt
- 1 tbsp dried oregano
- 3 garlic cloves minced
- For the potatoes:
- 4 large gold potatoes diced
- 1 lemon zested and juiced
- 1 zucchini diced
- ¼ red onion sliced
- 1 lemon quartered
- Crumbled feta for serving

Procedure:

- Make the marinade. In a large bowl, combine the lemon juice, lemon zest, ghee, salt, dried oregano, and garlic cloves. Add the chicken thighs and toss to evenly coat. Refrigerate and marinate for 1 Hour, or up to 12 Hours.
- Preheat the Air Fryer to 385°F / 195°C. Place chicken in the air fryer skin side up and cook for 15-16 Minutes, or until the skin is golden brown. Set aside.
- In a large mixing bowl, toss together the potatoes, lemon zest, lemon juice, zucchini, red onion slices, and quartered lemons.
- Place in the air fryer basket and Air Fry at 385°F / 195°C for another 15 Minutes, or until lightly golden and fragrant. Serve alongside chicken with a sprinkle of feta. Enjoy!

45 Minutes

Serves 4

PEACE OVER PAIN

RIBS IN ROASTED SALSA

Ingredients:

- 4 large Saladette tomatoes
- ½ onion cut into chunks
- 2 cloves garlic
- 3 serrano peppers or more
- 2 tbsp or cubes vegetable broth
- ½ bunch cilantro + 3 tbsp finely chopped for garnishing
- ½ cup Water
- 3 lb (1.5 kg) ribs
- Salt and pepper to taste
- Ghee

Procedure:

- Roast the tomatoes, onion chunks, garlic, and chiles. Let brown well, until skin looks moderately brown. Blend everything along with the broth, cilantro, and water.
- Season the ribs with salt and pepper.
- Place the stainless steel inner pot inside the pressure cooker. Press Saute and when Hot appears, add ghee and put the ribs in. Let brown on all sides. If necessary, do so in parts so as not to pile up the meat. Once the ribs are seared, add the sauce. Bring to a boil, check the amount of salt, and press Cancel.
- Close and lock the pressure cooker. Make sure the steam release handle is turned to sealing. Press Meat/Stew, pressure level High, and set time to 20 Minutes.
- Serve, sprinkle with fresh cilantro and enjoy.

130

6 Minutes

Serves 3

LENTIL STEW

Ingredients:

- 3 tbsp of ghee
- 1 chive finely sliced
- 2 cups Broccoli raw and chopped
- ½ zucchini sliced and quartered
- 1 cup oriental lentils red
- 1½ cups Water
- 2 tsp salt
- ½ tsp garlic powder

Procedure:

- Place the stainless steel inner pot inside the pressure cooker and add the ghee, green onion, broccoli, and zucchini. Press Saute, pressure level High, for 5 Minutes. Stir constantly to prevent burning.
- Add the lentils, water, salt, and garlic powder. Stir. Close and lock the pressure cooker lid. Make sure the steam release handle is turned to Sealing. Press Pressure Cook, pressure level Medium, and set time to 1 Minute.
- When done cooking, press Cancel. Then turn the steam release handle to Venting. Once all steam has been released, open the lid.

PERUVIAN CHICKEN STEW

Ingredients:

- 1 shredded chicken breast parboiled to medium
- 1 garlic minced
- 1 white onion chopped
- 1 tbsp ají amarillo paste
- 1 tsp nutmeg
- 1 tsp turmeric
- GF bread, toasted
- 1 can evaporated milk
- ½ cup chicken stock
- hard-boiled eggs to serve as garnish
- pecans
- Boiled potatoes

Procedure:

- Place the stainless steel inner pot inside the pressure cooker. Press Saute and set time to 12 Minutes. Sauté the onion.
- All the flavors will be incorporated in this sofrito.
- Add the ají amarillo (Peruvian yellow pepper), nutmeg, garlic, and turmeric.
- Add the parboiled chicken breast to the pressure cooker.
- Add the milk blended with the bread and season with salt.
- Close and lock the pressure cooker. Make sure the steam release handle is turned to Sealing. Press Pressure Cook, pressure level High, and set time to 10 Minutes.
- Serve with boiled potatoes, eggs, and pecans.

25 Minutes

Serves 8

PEACE OVER PAIN

FISH STEW

Ingredients:

- 4 fish fillets
- 1 tsp of ghee
- Salt, pepper, cumin
- 1 tbsp garlic paste
- 2 tbsp ají amarillo paste
- 2 tbsp aji panca paste
- 2 tbsp red wine vinegar
- 1 cup fish broth or water
- 6 potatoes or 2 lb (1 kg) cassava, peeled
- 2 large red onions
- 4 tomatoes
- 1 aji amarillo (Peruvian yellow pepper)
- Some parsley sprigs
- Some cilantro sprigs

Procedure:

- Season the fish fillets with salt and pepper.
- In the bowl of the pressure cooker put a tsp of ghee put the Saute function and set the time to 7 Minutes.
- Heat the ghee and add the garlic paste, yellow chili, panca chili, salt, pepper, cumin, red vinegar and Saute well.
- Add the fish broth, the potatoes or cassava peeled into not very small pieces, on top of these we put the fish fillets and on top the onion cut as for sweating, the tomato cut into wedges, the seedless yellow chili cut into thin strips, the parsley and coriander.
- Place and lock the lid of the pressure cooker making sure the steam release valve is turned to "sealing". Set the function to Soup/Broth and set the time to 3 Minutes.
- Accompany with white rice.

BONE BROTH

Ingredients:

- 4 pounds meaty beef stock bones with lots of marrow and knuckle bones
- 1 pound stew meat and/or beef scraps cut into 2-inch chunks, chuck or flank steak
- 1 tbsp of ghee
- 1 medium onions quartered
- 1 large carrots cut into 1 to 2-inch chunks
- 1 large celery rib cut into 1-inch segments or handful celery tops
- 3 garlic cloves unpeeled, smashed
- handful fresh parsley including stems and leaves
- 2 bay leaves
- 8-10 peppercorns

Procedure:

- Preheat oven to 400°F. Rub a little bit of ghee over the stew meat. Place stock bones and stew meat into the Cooking Vessel.
- Once the oven has preheated, place the Cooking Vessel into the oven. Roast in the oven for about 45 minutes. Turn the bones and meat pieces half-way through cooking, until nicely browned.
- When the bones and meat are nicely browned, remove the Cooking Vessel from the oven and place it into the Cooking Base.
- Add carrots, onions celery tops, garlic, parsley, bay leaves and peppercorns into the Cooking Vessel.
- Fill with cold water, 2 inches over the top of the bones (about 8-9 cups of water).
- **Continue on next page...**

134

12 Hours

stock

PEACE OVER PAIN

BONE BROTH

Procedure Continued:

- Close the lid. Select-SLOW COOK and set the time to 12 hours. Press START.
- From time to time check in on the stock and use a large metal spoon to scoop away the fat and any scum that rises to the surface.
- Do not stir the stock while cooking. Stirring will mix the fats in with the stock, clouding up the stock.
- Once the cooking cycle is complete, open the lid.
- Strain the beef stock through strainer.
- Serve immediately or let cool to room temperature then chill in the refrigerator. If you plan to freeze the stock, however, remove and discard the fat, pour the stock into a jar or plastic container.

GARLIC CRAYFISH

Ingredients:

- 1 lb (500 g) crayfish peeled and rinsed
- ½ onion diced
- 1 small head garlic (10 cloves garlic) chopped
- 2 tomatoes peeled and diced
- 1 cup crayfish shell or fish broth
- 3 tbsp ají amarillo puréed, Peruvian yellow pepper
- chopped cilantro
- Optional: chopped ají limo lemon drop pepper

Procedure:

- Place the inner pot inside the pressure cooker. Press Saute and set time to 15 Minutes. Add the onion and garlic until golden brown.
- Add the tomatoes and ají amarillo. Sauté lightly and add the crayfish. Change the setting to Meat/Stew, set time to 5 Minutes. Add the broth, cilantro and ají limo (optional).
- Lastly, serve with rice or other side dish of your choice.

50 Minutes

Serves 4

Flank Steak With Cranberry-Raspberry Salsa

Ingredients:

- ¼ cup chili sauce
- 3 dash hot sauce
- 1 ¼ oz taco seasoning
- 4 tbsp lime juice
- ¾ cup scallion sliced
- ½ cup fresh cilantro
- 1 tbsp Jalapeño seeded chopped
- 1 tbsp lime juice
- 1 tsp ground cumin
- 12 oz cranberry-raspberry crushed fruit crushed
- fresh cilantro as needed
- 2 lb flank steak trimmed
- 16 GF Flour Tortilla

Procedure:

- Combine lime juice, chili sauce, hot pepper sauce and taco seasoning in the inner pot of your pressure cooker.
- Add steak to pot, turning to coat.
- Slow cook on More for 1 Hour.
- Slow cook on Less for 9 Hours.
- While steak cooks, place scallions, cilantro sprigs, and jalapeño pepper in a food processor; pulse 5 times or until finely chopped.
- Add remaining lime juice, cumin, and cranberry-raspberry crushed fruit; process until smooth.
- Spoon mixture into a bowl; cover and chill.
- When slow cook time is up, remove steak from cooker; discard cooking liquid.
- Shred steak into bite-sized pieces, and garnish with cilantro, if desired.
- Warm tortillas according to package directions.
- Spread about 1 1/2 tablespoons salsa over each tortilla.
- Spoon about 1/2 cup shredded steak down center of each tortilla; roll up and serve.

BEEF STEW

Ingredients:

- 1.3 kg stew beef cut into chunks
- 2 yellow onion
- 5 clove garlic
- 1 liter beef stock
- 400 g Tinned tomatoes
- 1 tbsp fresh thyme
- 500 ml red wine
- 1 bay leaf
- 1 tbsp Worcestershire sauce
- 300 g carrot
- 400 g Baby potato
- 4 tbsp cornflour
- 1 tsp honey
- 5 g fresh parsley chopped
- Salt & pepper as needed
- 4 tbsp Water
- 1 tbsp of ghee

Procedure:

- Select Sauté on your pressure cooker and set the pot to the highest heat setting.
- Once hot, drizzle some melted ghee into the base of your pot until it lightly covers the base.
- Add your beef and fry until golden brown on all sides. Do this in batches without overcrowding the pot to get a good, golden brown sear on the beef.
- While the beef is cooking, halve the onions and cut them into eighths.
- Once the beef has finished cooking, remove it from the pressure cooker and set aside until needed. Do not clean the pot, as the caramelized beef bits will give great flavor to your sauce.
- Add the onion chunks to the pot along with more ghee, then sauté the onions until slightly softened.
- Add the garlic and sauté for one minute more.
- **Continue on next page...**

138

40 Minutes

Serves 4

BEEF STEW

Procedure Continued...

- Add the beef stock to your pressure cooker and deglaze the base, by scraping the bottom of the pot with a wooden spoon, to release any cooked bits of food- this will make your sauce extra delicious, and prevent a "burn notice" signal.
- Add in picked fresh thyme leaves.
- Layer the following ingredients to prevent the pot yielding a burn notice. On top of the onions place the beef cubes, tinned tomatoes, red wine, bayleaf, Worcestershire sauce and a generous pinch of salt and pepper. Do not stir, as this will cause the tomatoes to sink to the bottom and burn during pressure cooking.
- Secure the lid of the pressure cooker, select Pressure Cook and High Pressure, then set the timer to 30 Minutes. When the time is up, carefully quick release the pressure.
- While the beef cooks, peel the carrots, and dice them into bite sized chunks. Wash and halve the baby potatoes. Pour some of the remaining red wine into a glass and put your feet up.
- Once the beef has finished cooking and pressure is released, open the lid add in the carrots and halved baby potatoes.
- Secure the lid back on the pot, select Pressure Cook and High Pressure, then set the timer to 5 Minutes. When the time is up, carefully quick release the pressure and remove the lid.
- Mix the corn flour with water and store into a slurry.
- Pour this into the stew, along with the honey, and cook the stew on the setting until thickened.
- Season the stew to taste with salt and pepper, then serve nice and hot, alongside your favorite side with freshly chopped parsley.

CHICKEN MACARONI AND CHEESE

Ingredients:

- 2 boneless, skinless chicken breasts diced into 2 inch cubes
- Salt as needed
- Pepper as needed
- 4 tbsp unsalted butter
- 1 yellow onion minced
- 4 garlic cloves minced
- 3 ½ cups chicken broth
- ¾ cup sundried tomatoes diced
- 1 lb GF pasta
- 450 ml cream cheese
- 1 cup Parmesan cheese
- 2 cup shredded sharp white cheddar cheese
- 1 tbsp fresh oregano minced
- 1 cup cream
- 4 cups spinach leaves

Procedure:

- Sprinkle the diced chicken breast liberally with salt and pepper. Turn on the Sauté function at 320°F for 15 Minutes. Melt the butter in the pot. Brown the chicken on all sides, working in batches so as to not overcrowd the pot. Return all chicken back to the pot.
- Add the minced onion and garlic and sauté until fragrant, about 5 additional minutes.
- Add the chicken broth, diced sundried tomatoes, and penne pasta. Stir to evenly coat all noodles.
- Place the lid on top and Slow Cook on High for 2 Hours, or on Low for 3 ½ -4 Hours.
- After 30 Minutes of slow cooking on high, remove the lid and stir the pasta. Return the lid on the pot and continue cooking.
- After 1 Hour, add the cream cheese, sharp cheese, and parmesan cheese. Stir to combine. Place the lid on and continue cooking until time is over.
- Once the pasta has cooked, mix in the oregano and cream. Fold in the spinach and keep warm until wilted. Serve immediately.

60 Minutes

Serves 8

ANCHO CHILE PORK TENDERLOIN

Ingredients:

- 2 tbsp ancho chili powder
- 1 tbsp ground cumin
- 1 tbsp salt
- 1 tbsp freshly ground black peppercorn
- 1 orange juice and zested
- 1 tbsp honey
- 1 tbsp ghee
- 1 ¼ lb pork tenderloin

Procedure:

- Make the marinade. In a large mixing bowl, combine the chili powder, ground cumin, salt, black peppercorn, orange juice, orange zest, honey, and ghee. Place the tenderloin in the mixing bowl and rub the marinade on all sides. Refrigerate and marinate for at least 2 Hours, or up to 36 Hours.
- Preheat the Air Fryer to 400°F / 205°C. Shake off any excess marinade and air fry the pork tenderloin for 8 minutes.
- Reduce the air fryer temperature to 325°F / 160°C. Air fry for another 5-8 Minutes, or until the internal temperature of the thickest part of the tenderloin reads 140°F.
- Let the pork tenderloin rest for 10 Minutes before slicing. Cut into pieces and serve with your favorite side!

4 Hours

8 Cups

MULLED APPLE CIDER

Ingredients:

- 6 honey crisp apples quartered and deseeded
- 6 granny smith apples quartered and deseeded
- 8 cups Water
- 4 cinnamon sticks
- 4 star anise
- 1 tbsp whole cloves
- 1 large orange sliced
- ½ cup brown sugar

Procedure:

- Place all ingredients except the brown sugar in the pot.
- Place the lid on top and Slow Cook on High for 4 Hours, or on Low for 8 Hours.
- After the time is done, mash the fruit to disperse more flavor.
- Strain all the solids and liquids through a fine mesh strainer into a large mixing bowl. Discard the solids. Return the cider back to the pot on the Warm setting for a hot drink, or cool, refrigerate,and serve over ice.

142

15 Minutes

4 Servings

PEACE OVER PAIN

HONEY GARLIC PORK CHOPS

Ingredients:

- 4 Bone -in pork chops
- 1 tbsp honey
- 2 Garlic clove
- 1 lemon
- 1 tbsp ghee
- Salt as needed
- Black pepper as needed

Procedure:

- In a small bowl combine the honey, mashed garlic, ghee, and lemon juice.
- Brush the honey garlic sauce over the pork chops. Season generously with salt and pepper.
- Place the pork chops on air fryer basket, careful not to overlap. Cook in batches if necessary.
- Air Fry at 400°F/205°C for 11-13 Minutes turning over halfway. Pork chops are done when the internal temperature reaches 145°F, and the outside is golden and seared.
- Let the pork chops rest for at least 5 Minutes. Cut into slices and serve.

DR. REESE'S SIMPLE MAN RECIPES

No Idea

No Idea

DR. REESE'S BURGER POTATO THING

Ingredients:

- 2 beef patties
- 1 sweet potato
- A handful of broccoli or asparagus

Procedure:

- Pour water into a pan and make sure it's about a half an inch all the way around
- Skin and cut up potatoes into small pieces, place in pot and let boil/steam for about 5 minutes covered
- Then place 2 frozen burgers in the pot and boil/steam with the potatoes for another ten minutes covered
- Check your potatoes and burgers. Using your spatula, cut the burgers into smaller pieces to cook better
- Add your green stuff
- Let cook for another 5 minutes or so
- Drain water and enjoy

No Idea

No Idea

PEACE OVER PAIN

DR. REESE'S QUICK AVO EGGS

Ingredients:

- 4 cage free eggs
- 1 avocado

Procedure:

- Crack 4 eggs straight into a pan
- Cook on high for about a minute then lower to medium
- Use a wood or hard plastic spatula to mix the eggs (my version of beating them, it saves on washing another bowl)
- Turn off stove when you have a nice mixture of yellow and white
- Keep eggs in pan and let it cook without the flame
- Open an avocado, make sure there are no black or brown spots (oxidation)
- Dump the avocado onto a plate and add your cooked soft scrambled eggs. Add lots of salt

No Idea

No Idea

DR. REESE'S ROAST

Ingredients:

- 1 roast
- A package of organic carrots
- 1 clove of garlic
- Russet potatoes or whatever is on sale
- 1 Bag of frozen broccoli

Procedure:

- Pour water in the inner pot and make sure it's about an inch deep
- Dump the roast in and salt it good with my recommended salt
- Break the carrots with your hands if you're in a rush and throw them in
- Slice the garlic open so it's exposed and chuck it in
- Chop up as many potatoes that will fit
- Dump the bag of green stuff in
- Set the pressure cooker to the meat setting for 70 minutes.

DR. REESE'S BEEF STEW

Ingredients:

- 2 packages of beef chunks
- A package of organic carrots
- 1 clove of garlic
- Russet potatoes or whatever is on sale
- 1 Bag of frozen broccoli

Procedure:

- Pour water in the inner pot of pressure cooker and make sure it's about an inch deep
- Dump the beef chunks in and salt them good with my recommended salt
- Break the carrots with your hands if you're in a rush and throw them in
- Slice the garlic open so it's exposed and chuck it in
- Chop up as many potatoes that will fit
- Dump the bag of green stuff in
- Set the pressure cooker to the meat setting for 45 minutes. It's all about to smell good soon.

No Idea

No Idea

PEACE OVER PAIN

DR. REESE'S CHICKEN THIGHS

Ingredients:

- 1 package of chicken thighs
- Salt

Procedure:

- Pour water in the inner pot of pressure cooker and make sure it's about an inch deep
- Dump the chicken thighs in
- Salt the thighs as much as possible
- Set the pressure cooker to poultry/meat and set it for 45 minutes
- You may use the water after as stock for another recipe

DR. REESE'S GF PIZZA

Ingredients:

- 1 GF pizza from Aldi's
- 1 turkey burger
- Greek yogurt

Procedure:

- Keep Aldi pizza in fridge, then place in oven for 15 minutes on 330F
- Boil a turkey burger on the stove top for 10 minutes
- Use a wood or hard plastic spatula to then cut up the burger into small pieces, let it cook for another 3-5 minutes
- Drain water on your burger, take out pizza and add burger pieces onto the pizza
- Add as much greek yogurt as you desire and enjoy - Note, it will be a flimsy pizza and not crispy. More like a calzone if you fold it

No Idea

No Idea

PEACE OVER PAIN

DR. REESE'S NACHOS

Ingredients:

- 1 box of mary's original crackers or 1 box of flackers
- 1 box of black beans
- Greek yogurt
- Avocado
- White Shredded cheese

Procedure:

- Boil your black beans for about 5 minutes
- Add your beans and avocado into a bowl and mash them
- Add as much greek yogurt as you desire
- Add salt and any other seasoning you wish
- Add shredded cheese if you'd like
- Dip the crackers - go to town

No Idea

No Idea

PEACE OVER PAIN

DR. REESE'S POPCORN TREAT

Ingredients:

- Organic popcorn
- Air popper machine
- Ghee or organic butter
- High quality salt
- Nutritional Yeast (optional for cheesy taste)

Procedure:

- Dump a bunch of kernels in the popping machine and hit start
- Put as much ghee or butter as you desire in a pan and turn on the stove top for about 1 minute, don't let it burn
- Take out the biggest bowl you can find
- Pour popcorn in bowl and drizzle the ghee/butter all over the popcorn
- Add as much salt as you can tolerate
- Shake the bowl
- Eat then repeat until you're full
- When you get full, take blood sugar nutrients to help metabolize all the sugar
- Dr. Reese eats this 1x per week as lunch

NEED TO HEAL?

The first step in healing the body is to discover the root causes behind your symptoms.

So I developed a new and unique head-to-toe process called the HEAD TO TOE ANALYSIS.

This one of a kind consultation reveals root causes which saves you thousands of dollars on blood, urine, stool and hair labs. Not to mention radiation filled x-rays and trips to multiple medical monopoly physicians.

It can be a liberating experience as you receive the answers your medical monopoly doctor couldn't give you.

When I'm evaluating your body I'm looking at your pelvic position, shoulder position, neck position, head position, feet health and spinal health. There are so many symptoms that come from being out of alignment. For example, you could have chronic migraines and allergies because of your neck and head position. Or you could have sciatica because of your pelvis position. Or you could have a bulging disk because of your foot position. Everything is connected.
By seeing what's out of alignment, we know what corrective exercise protocols to give you in order to get the muscles functioning which would bring your bones back to normal and promote healing.

I'm also checking your stomach acid levels. Without proper stomach acid, which should be like battery acid, you can not digest food properly. When you can't digest well, two bad things happen.
1- The food ferments and causes bloating and belching. Eventually, it will start to shoot back up your esophagus like a volcano. This is typically called acid reflux. If it happens often, it's called GERD. And if you let that go for decades, that turns into the c-monster.
2- The food isn't being broken down enough so it's going into your small intestine too big in size which creates more malabsorption. This of course can lead to nutritional deficiency which brings forth up to 900 symptoms.

Speaking of nutritional deficiency, I would be evaluating which categories you're lacking in. There are four categories. Hard tissue, soft tissue, blood sugar and digestive. I can figure out which categories are good or bad through the science of symptomatology.

This means that over the last 200 years it has been documented which symptoms mean what. So a simple intake questionnaire works well for this. For example, if you're having chronic nightmares, I know it's a blood sugar deficiency. If you have early onset gray hair, I know it's soffit tissue deficiency.

Each category receives a numbered score. If you have a 5 or over in any category, you're in rough shape. If you score a 4, then you're on the verge of being in rough shape. These numbers tell me what your nutritional protocol will need to be and what supplements need to be ordered.

The real magic of the discovery analysis is when I connect the dots. If someone is suffering from parkinsons and their neck is severely forward I know it's a root cause because the head is not draining fluid properly. Also, if they don't have enough stomach acid, I know it's a root cause because now the fats may not be getting to the brain. I can also make an educated guess that there could be pinched nerves.

If someone has bone spurs in their feet, I can see if it's coming from their hip position which is affecting their gait (walking pattern). I can also see if they're deficient in the hard tissue category.

It's my opinion that this discovery analysis is the most effective way to view what's wrong with a human-being. No one is doing this (yet) and every human needs it so they can get the answers they need. More importantly, so solution protocols can be put into place.

My discovery (no pun) is that there can be multiple root causes to one issue. I laid this out in my book, PEACE OVER PAIN toward the end and will do it in more detail in this book. It's key for you to understand that there is no absolute way to know what your causes are exactly. It could be 1 of 7 root causes or 7 of 7 making your back hurt.

The beauty in all this is, it doesn't matter!

My reversal system was developed to go after all the root causes at one time.

Then you escape a life of pain and drugs.

www.DRKEVINREESE.com

Made in the USA
Las Vegas, NV
07 April 2025

20684723R00090